Lived Space

Jakob Egholm Feldt
Kirstine Sinclair
(eds.)

Lived Space

Reconsidering Transnationalism
among Muslim Minorities

PETER LANG

Frankfurt am Main · Berlin · Bern · Bruxelles · New York · Oxford · Wien

Bibliographic Information published by the Deutsche Nationalbibliothek
The Deutsche Nationalbibliothek lists this publication in the Deutsche Nationalbibliografie; detailed bibliographic data is available in the internet at http://dnb.d-nb.de.

Cover Design:
Olaf Gloeckler, Atelier Platen, Friedberg

This publication has received financial support
from Institute for Cross-Cultural and Regional Studies,
University of Copenhagen; Institute for Culture and Identity,
Roskilde University; Faculty of Humanities,
University of Southern Denmark.

ISBN 978-3-631-60071-9
© Peter Lang GmbH
Internationaler Verlag der Wissenschaften
Frankfurt am Main 2011
All rights reserved.

All parts of this publication are protected by copyright. Any utilisation outside the strict limits of the copyright law, without the permission of the publisher, is forbidden and liable to prosecution. This applies in particular to reproductions, translations, microfilming, and storage and processing in electronic retrieval systems.

www.peterlang.de

Table of Contents

Lived Space: Reconsidering Transnationalism among Muslim Minorities
Jakob Egholm Feldt & Kirstine Sinclair 7

Re-considering Trans-Nationalism: Historical and Conceptual Reflections
Jakob Egholm Feldt 11

Between Gaza and Here: Analytical Reflections on Modes of
Identification, Minority Identity and Lived Space among Muslims in
Britain and Denmark in the Course of the Gaza Conflict 2008-09
Birgitte Schepelern Johansen & Dorthe Høvids Possing 29

Hizb ut-Tahrir and Notions of Home
Kirstine Sinclair 49

Spaces, Negotiation and Conflict: Muslim and Non-Muslim Encounters in
Nørrebro, Copenhagen
Garbi Schmidt 65

Whose Courtroom? Observations from Terrorism Trials
Ann-Sophie Hemmingsen 83

Trans-National Islamic TV: A Space for Religious and Gendered Living
Ehab Galal 99

The Exclusion of Denizens within the Irish Social and Political Opportunity
Structure: The Cosmopolitan Case of Muslims in the Republic of Ireland
Des Delaney and Francesco Cavatorta 123

List of Authors 155

Lived Space: Reconsidering Transnationalism among Muslim Minorities

Jakob Egholm Feldt & Kirstine Sinclair

With this anthology, we wish to explore the concept and practices of *Lived Space* among Muslim minorities in Europe. Our exploration will be guided by our mutual interest in concepts such as 'space/place', 'home', 'loyalty' and 'togetherness' and the way these sensibilities make individual and collective identities very real, located and concrete, and accordingly, constitute the substantive ground that binds people together. Thus, we consider this common bond to be basically sentimental but, nevertheless, it should be studied as a social fact making Muslim minorities located, grounded and rooted equal to other Westerners.

Lived Space is a phrase that we have borrowed from Tim Cresswell's excellent book *Place. A Short Introduction* and his introduction to *Mobilizing Place, Placing Mobility: The Politics of Representation in a Globalized World*. Cresswell himself has borrowed the phrase from Edward Soja and in many respects we share the ambition with both Cresswell and Soja to try to question or even overcome habitual dichotomies between place as a subjective emotional relation and place as an objective infrastructure. Thus, the phrase Lived Space, however intangible and even slightly contradictory, is the headline of an attempt to combine ontologies and epistemologies of space to form more integrated and thereby realistic accounts of Muslim life in Europe.

Space is usually understood as opposed to place. This makes much sense as space is usually considered a void or an extension while place is associated with names; identities. Thus, the dichotomies involved are classic: Unknown-known, universal-particular, extended-ended, strange-familiar, etc. Following this logic Lived Space points to an activity by which the unknown becomes known, the universal particular and the extended becomes ended and vice versa: The filling out of space with human relations, the making sense of space, the transformation of space into places with identities, the doing of the perpetual extensions and changes that occur in human spatial relations.

We have been inspired by recent books on critical cultural and human geography primarily the work of Tim Cresswell and Doreen Massey. We find that a very fruitful inter-disciplinarity can be established between cultural and religious studies of

Muslim minorities, European-Middle Eastern encounters, and human geography. Inevitably, studies of Muslim religious minorities in Europe and studies of European-Middle Eastern encounters entail a significant and even founding spatial extension or change. Almost by definition, studies of European-Middle Eastern encounters evolve along trails of extension or changes of geo-graphy, geo-strategy, and geo-policy. Studies of Muslim religious minorities are no less spatial and are subject to all the inherent meaning of the orders of European-Middle Eastern encounters. When we study and describe the ghettos, the neighbourhoods, the minority spaces and their transgressions of national and cultural borders, we also study the extensions and changes of spatial orders because spaces and places are essentially made up of human relations. Studies of Muslim religious minorities in Europe and European-Middle Eastern encounters are themselves completely intertwined as we experience increased mobility and integration between Europe and the Middle East.

What we have found to be the case in much literature on Muslim minorities in Europe is that the concept of transnationalism is often used to describe the commonsensical fact that individual and collective relations among Muslim minorities very often cross state borders – hence transnational. In this use of transnationalism is implied the a priori assumption that border crossing is a particular quality. In principle, it counts for all transgressors but in Europe to Muslims more than to other religious minorities or majorities the last 15-20 years. Often, the qualitative dimension of transnationalism is presented as some sort of vantage point or positive potential as seen in theoretical work by Edward Said, Arjun Appadurai or Peter Mandaville. At other times, in Olivier Roy's and Gilles Kepel's work for instance, it is presented as a potential problem for the social cohesion of the Europeans states, or as something particularly interesting to study because of the a priori difference implied when we discuss Muslim minorities. In any case, the general use of the concept of transnationalism in either its empirical or qualitative dimension fails to define transnationalism as a substantially meaningful concept pointing to new understandings that are not already implied in most globalisation literature since the beginning of the 1990s. Nevertheless, the concept of transnationalism should not be rejected but rather re-qualified through a reconsideration of its potentials and limitations or through suggestions for completely new understandings of it.

Regarding the concepts of space/place, home, loyalty and togetherness interesting new perspectives for the study of Muslims in Europe arise from the indeed very diverse theoretical work of among others Tim Cresswell, Doreen Massey, Richard Rorty, Lars-Henrik Schmidt, Mikhail Bakhtin, Wendy Brown, Slavoj Zizek and Chantal Mouffe, some recent and some classical theoretical sources. These authors, despite their significant differences, emphasise the need for integrating social science, psychoanalysis, philosophy, cultural studies and narratology in order to understand the complexity of 'the social' which Muslim minorities are part of and not parted from. The central concepts of the social that we wish to emphasise, space/place, home, loyalty, togetherness, are all both subjective and objective, empirical and sentimental, historical and still permanently in the making. The location of these senses can be mapped, they can be presented, imagined and embodied by people, and they are done, made, through the practice of living. Focusing on these concepts, we, following Cresswell, want to tune into the *lived space* of Muslim minorities in Europe.

The contributions to this book have two primary interests that are addressed in different ways. Firstly, they seek to find ways to describe *the spaces* that Muslim Europeans inhabit and *the places* that make (common) sense to them without ascribing any a priori difference, queerness, danger, or vanguard position to them. Secondly, the contributions critically engage with the concept of trans-nationalism which in many respects defines the predominant perspective on Muslim minorities in social and cultural analysis. In this way, the book is located between two concepts that are not readily compatible in as much as *Lived Space* as a perspective is sensitive to ontology while trans-nationalism most often is used analytically to add to or transform our knowledge about Muslims thus making epistemological claims. We find that this tension is very fruitful for our exploration of the common ground that binds Muslim groups together. Hence, we aim at integrating exploration of *being Muslim in Europe* with critical interventions into *explaining Muslims in Europe*.

We hope that the collection will make *lived space* more than a well-coined term and introduce new perspectives on the practice of living among Muslim minorities.

***

The anthology consists of chapters that either critically engage in the use of the concept of transnationalism in the study of Muslim minorities in Europe either theoretically or through original empirical research or present original research focusing on the making of place, home, senses of loyalty and togetherness among Muslim minorities in Europe.

The opening chapter of the volume by Jakob Egholm Feldt discusses the origins of the concepts of transnational and transnationalism and argues that the present day use of the concepts in social science analyses of minorities in the West very much supports a shift from sedentary to nomadic metaphysics. Chapter two by Possing and Johansen continues the investigation of these concepts in relation to Muslims in Britain. Here it is argued that the perspective of lived space contributes to the analysis of identification production in potential asymmetrical power relations between majority and minorities.

Identification as well as negotiation are central to the following four chapters. In chapter three, Sinclair analyses the connection between a transnational political ideology setting the frame for engagement in politico-religious activities and concrete strategies for creating home and making sense of such activities in the everyday life of members of the Islamist organisation, Hizb ut-Tahrir. In chapter four, Schmidt analyses examples of identity negotiations through different use of public space. The relationality of space is central to the argument here – what people do and how a given space is used can be expressions of opposition as well as belonging. In chapter five, Hemmingsen looks at a very specific place, namely the court room. Using Danish terror court cases as illustration, she argues that no place is neutral, and that even a court room becomes a stage for negotiations over the right to belong. Even the court room offers oppositional agendas to be lived. The following chapter, Galal's chapter six, analyses satellite TV programmes as lived space. The argument is that through life style programmes and programmes of religious content female audiences gain the opportunity to self-identify and participate in gender debates to further extent than previously seen. Finally, chapter seven by Delaney and Cavatorta, discusses the conditions for Muslims in the Republic of Ireland in terms of political participation. The idea here is to investigate the background for the development of a distinct cosmopolitanism amongst the Muslims minorities present in the country. Again, questions concerning identification, negotiation and belonging are central to the argument.

We have attempted to reach a degree of convergence of concepts and perspectives through discussion of ideas and presentations in two seminars. One at University of Southern Denmark in November 2008 and one in March 2009 at the Danish Institute for Social Research with the purpose of framing our *Erkenntnisinteressen* and aligning our contributions. The seminars have been held under the auspices of FIFO, the Danish Association for Research on Islam and Muslims, and we wish to thank FIFO, its board and in particular chairman Garbi Schmidt for supporting this project all the way. We would also like to thank the anonymous reviewers from *Tidsskrift for Islamforskning* (Journal of Islam Research) and the research group on Cultural History at Roskilde University for helpful comments and suggestions.

We are grateful for the financial support from the following institutions:

− Faculty of Humanities, University of Southern Denmark
− Institute for Cross-Cultural and Regional Studies, University of Copenhagen
− Institute for Culture and Identity, Roskilde University

Re-considering Trans-Nationalism: Historical and Conceptual Reflections

Jakob Egholm Feldt

Introduction[1]

In recent years the concept of the trans-national, or trans-nationalism, has become widely used in various branches of social and humanistic research. Its use is included in vocabularies of the study of ideas, people, and commodities across nation state borders where the objects of study are qualified by the fact that they go across nations and states. Ideas, people, and commodities have always crossed various cultural and state lines but it seems that the recent focus on 'border crossing' is concerned with three aspects in particular: 1. Objects that are *qualitatively* trans-national, 2. The 'box' that contains 'society' meaning that the nation and the state are inadequate boxes (categories) in which to find evident aspects of 'society' such as global commodities, migrants and different popular cultural trends, 3. Writing or analyzing from a trans-national perspective or attitude. Accordingly, the recent widespread use of the concept of 'the trans-national', or trans-nationalism, has both ontological and epistemological concerns that are relevant to scrutinize in some detail. Here, I will discuss the concept of trans-nationalism in, mostly implicit, relation to the recent popularity of the concept in the fields of history, cultural studies and research on Muslim minorities in Europe. The discussion will take as a point of departure a brief historicizing of the idea of the trans-national. Following the trail of the idea of the trans-national since the beginning of the 20th century will give us an impression of the layers of uses and meanings that this idea or perspective has had over time. It is my contention that these layers bear upon the meaning(s) of today's use of the concept and, furthermore, it seems that most scholars have not paid attention to this legacy. This might seem a little odd considering the fact that in particular the study of Muslim minorities has been at the center of political and scholarly controversies over ideological leanings in scholarship and more or less direct partisan involvement of scholars on behalf of Muslim minorities and/or immigrants. At the same time scholars

---

1 Thanks to students at Roskilde University who assisted me in studying and understanding the material used in this paper: Astrid Andersen, Ditte Jensen, Emil Ulrichsen, Nadia Christensen, Signe Madsen and Sigridur Jonsdottir.

have often criticized hard-liner policies on minorities and immigration. Such policies are popular in most if not all European countries and have been increasingly so the last 15-20 years. Thus, it seems reasonable to ask whether or not the concept of trans-nationalism carries with it meanings that in some way or another valorize what Tim Cresswell calls *a nomadic metaphysics* (Cresswell, 2006, p. 26).

The Trans-National

The concept of the 'trans-national' is about 100 years old. As far as I have been able to detect, it appears for the first time in Randolph Bourne's 1916 article *Trans-National America* (R. Bourne, 1916). Bourne was part of the intellectual, pragmatist movement around philosophers and public intellectuals William James, John Dewey and Horace M. Kallen who have inspired later cosmopolitanism, liberalism and progressivism. To Bourne, trans-nationalism is an attitude, a way of thinking in opposition to the well-known American melting pot ideology that seeks to melt cultures into *a culture* namely American Culture. It is about seeing the world as it really is namely a *federation of national colonies* (America is a world federation in miniature) and a plea against sentimentalizing and moralizing history. And significantly, trans-nationalism is set against European 'old-fashioned' nationalism by Bourne who looked to Europe and the First World War to see the crumbling of the old world and to America to see the dawning of the new. Trans-nationalism is nationalism without universalism, essentialism, and sovereignty: Inter-national solidarity.

Bourne and his circle were interested not only in coining a new concept for a tolerant family of nations but also in creating an entire new philosophy that could relate the individual to the collective and vice versa in a modern and rational manner. They all emphasized different levels of abstraction of this new philosophy of transnationalism but they were united in both the pragmatist origins of their thinking, and in the end goal of their ideological vision. But as in all close circles they had heated arguments over all sorts of details. Bourne was primarily occupied with founding a new political, transnational discourse; James was interested in subjective, philosophical and psychological aspects of the new humanism that was the common ground beneath trans-nationalism, while John Dewey became one of the 20th century most significant progressive educational philosophers. Horace M. Kallen was also concerned with progressive educational development as one of the cornerstones of what he called cultural pluralism. Kallen developed the key idea that cultural pluralism and nationalism was not necessarily each other's opposites in 1915 which Bourne in 1916 turned into the main point of his programmatic article "Trans-National America" (R. Bourne, 1916; Horace M Kallen, 1915).

The philosophical foundations of the ideology of trans-nationalism were laid by philosopher Charles Sanders Peirce (1839-1914). Peirce is today widely recognized as maybe the greatest of American philosophers and his philosophy is central to fields such as pragmatics and general semiotics. Here, I will not go into details of the importance of Peirce to the new ideas of the subject and of perception that James, Dewey, Bourne and Kallen developed into a full blown progressive American thinking on the relation between the individual, culture, the nation and international relations. It will suffice for our purposes here to note that out of Peirce's complicated and diverse thinking James, Dewey, Bourne, Kallen and other later pragmatists emphasized Peirce's scientific rationality, his theory of signs and his fundamentally anti-metaphysical attitude. Peirce claimed among many other things that sign, object and interpretant are interrelated. We cannot understand one without the other. In Peirce, experience is the teacher. We constantly control and modify our understandings through experience while we strive to remove doubt that unsettles our beliefs. To Peirce, belief is the foundation of action by which he does not mean religious belief but what we in common sense would call knowledge. Doubt on the other hand is a temporary unpleasant condition, a standstill that we by different types of inference rush to get out of (Peirce, 1877). The Peircian logic was by early 20th century progressives interpreted (and misinterpreted) into a type of cultural and political ideology, and normative educational programs (Mounce, 2002).

James, Dewey and others used Peirce as a source for arguing for a more relativistic and epistemological understanding of man (Dewey, 1999; James, 1990). Because man acts on his conceptions and beliefs but is taught by experience they emphasized emotions and sensibilities as arenas for change. The change of emotions and sensibilities was necessary because it would bring new conceptions and possibilities to the experience of suffering and hardships in America and Europe apart from war. Just as sign, object and interpretant is a cluster that must be understood in its totality as a *relation*, man and the world are to be considered a relation continuously created in a semiotic process. Accordingly, the progressive cultural and political philosophy conceived of man as an interpreter and builder of his own world. There were and still are three levels of abstraction to this philosophy namely that (1) man is interpretive, (2) humanism is not about a common meaning or essence of Man but about recognizing common semiotic and cultural processes, (3) rational political thought and behavior must take the semiotic and cultural processes into account when creating everything from public school education to international organizations.

Randolph Bourne articulated the radicality of the trans-national perspective most clearly in his essay of 1916 when he advocated an abolition of historical hierarchies. Bourne simply suggested the giving up of the idea of "the indigenous". We are all or were all once colonizers:

> We are all foreign-born or the descendants of foreign-born, and if distinctions are to be made between us they should rightly be on some other ground than indigenousness. The early colonists came over with motives no less colonial than the later. They did not come to be assimilated in an American melting-pot. They did not come to adopt the culture of the American Indian. They had not the smallest intention of "giving themselves without reservation" to the new country. They came to get freedom to live as they wanted. They came to escape from the stifling air and chaos of the old world; they came to make their fortune in a new land. They invented no new social framework. Rather they brought over bodily the old ways to which they had been accustomed. Tightly concentrated on a hostile frontier, they were conservative beyond belief. Their pioneer daring was reserved for the objective conquest of material resources. In their folkways, in their social and political institutions, they were, like every colonial people, slavishly imitative of the mother-country (R. Bourne, 1916, p. 88).

Bourne wished to make it clear that immigrants cannot be blamed for not wanting to assimilate. They do not travel to another part of the world to become somebody different but to be free to live as they wish. Therefore, it is not the fault of the Germans, the Scandinavians or the Italians that the melting pot is not working; it is because there is a wrong idea of Americanism. In effect, Bourne suggested a reflexive community of people who always come from somewhere else. People who had the right to live in the spirit of their mytho-historical origins but recognized this right as a foundational condition of their new community of cultural difference. Bourne envisioned a community of diversity where nations could mingle without being homogenized:

> It is the vague historic idealisms which have provided the fuel for the European flame. Our American ideal can make no progress until we do away with this romantic gilding of the past. All our idealisms must be those of future social goals in which all can participate, the good life of personality lived in the environment of the Beloved Community (R. Bourne, 1916, p. 97).

Here Bourne does away with the organic past and conditions the good life in our respective ethnocentric communities, in future social goals for all. The very possibility of living well with our own people is tied to a common future goal for the community of Man; or the community of communities. As previously mentioned, trans-nationalism's political goal is inter-national solidarity both within and between nations and nation-states.

Contextualizing Trans-Nationalism

There is no doubt that the concept of trans-nationalism arose out of dramatic political and social contexts. Bourne and his circle were intensely occupied with primarily two pressing political and social issues of their times namely increasing tension and ethnic conflict in America and World War I. In many respects, they considered these issues to be related and addressed them together as part of the founding of a new world vision. When considering the history and legacy of a concept, the events and experiences that gave rise to the concept in the first place play an important part in shaping its core meaning. In the texts by Bourne, Dewey and Kallen, the First World War and the crisis of the American melting pot were both problems related to romantic and idealistic conceptions and cultural practices of the nation and nationalism. In this period, there was considerable dissatisfaction among the older generations of Americans with the attitudes and seeming lack of interest in becoming American of recent immigrants from Europe.

> It is in the area where Scandinavians are most concentrated that Norwegian is preached on Sunday in more churches than in Norway. That area is Minnesota, not unlike Scandinavia in climate and character. There, if the newspapers are to be trusted, the "foreign language" taught in an increasingly larger number of high schools is Scandinavian. The Constitution of the State resembles in many respects the famous Norwegian Constitution of 1813. The largest city has been chosen as the "spiritual capital", if I may say so, the seat of the Scandinavian "house of life", which the Scandinavian Society in America is reported to be planning to build as a center from which there is to spread through the land Scandinavian culture and ideals (Horace M Kallen, 1915, p. 217).

Kallen gave a number of such examples to the point that all over America parallel societies were being developed in which people were more Norwegian than in Norway or more Jewish than in the ghetto. The older generation of Americans began organizing in historical and moral societies for upholding the true spirit of Americanism and many criticized the separatist behavior of the immigrants.

The liberal pragmatist circles considered this development a threat to American democracy and in the end a danger that America would slide into the state of Europe with its perpetual conflicts between nations and nation-states. World War I was very much seen by these circles as the culmination of rampant nationalism and sentimental historical feelings. So more than creating a fear of war itself or an explicit pacifism, the American, liberal experience of the world war created a fear that nationalism and its politics of history, identity and culture would lead also to the destruction of America. The magnitude of the European disaster and the necessity of American involvement led American liberals to recognize that any genuine solution to the problem of nationalism had to be global in perspective but local in its practical implementation. Accordingly, people such as Bourne, Dewey and Kallen were vigorously involved in discussions of global policy making before, during and after the world war but they all emphasized the significance of the individual subject and his/her learning processes on an everyday basis. It was the fundamental understandings of the individual subject; its foundational metaphysics that needed to be amended towards recognition of the perpetual semiosis that makes up human understanding. Europe was the proof that this change away from history and belonging was not only scientifically and philosophically legitimate but also plainly politically necessary. Europeans looked to history and belonging in a restorative perspective which considered the past a better place while the present was the expression of a degeneration of historical character and virtues. The future was a dystopia where the nation was being desecrated by internal others such as Jews, Gypsies, artists, homosexuals, or other queer or trans-categories, or threatened by competing nations from the outside. Often both were the case which led to rapidly increasing cultural and political tension in Europe in the decades preceding the First World War.

The liberal pragmatist circles identified the restorative perspective to be the heart of the problem and not the feelings of belonging and happiness among one's own people. Therefore, they insisted that the future is the goal of any progressive, peace seeking, social politics or even philosophy. The future had to include a social hope for Man; a hope of peace and human solidarity otherwise there would ultimately be endless efforts of mutual destruction as exemplified by the world war. Charles Sanders Peirce's original theory of signs and semiosis was interpreted into a much wider redemptive philosophy of the permanent process of renewal of Man; of a permanent individual, subjective and cultural learning process.

Summing up, we find that the transnational was coined in the context of three primary influences. The first and foundational influence is philosophical and it can generally be ascribed to Peirce, James and the gradual evolution of a pragmatist perspective in American philosophy, psychology and social thinking. Secondly, trans-nationalism was born of increasing social strife in America over immigration. The third influence was the American experience of the First World War and its implicit call for a new world order in which America should play a leading role due to its cultural pluralism. The concept of the trans-national includes in its first meaning an idea of the subject as a learning process; a new liberal, pragmatic humanism which was different from the German *Bildung* humanism; and a political and social goal of nationalism without essentialism: Inter-national solidarity on both global and local scale.

Culture – and the Symphony of Man

In understanding trans-nationalism and the trans-national perspective, the at the time increasingly important concept culture is worthwhile looking into. In the decades up to and immediately after World War I, culture developed further from the ethnographic classification system originating in Johann Gottfried Herder's thinking. Culture's significance for nationalism is almost a truism in today's historical and cultural research but what is much less noticed is that the concept of culture played and plays an equally crucial role in non-nationalist and progressive perspectives. What is important for our purposes here is to show how culture was a Janus-faced concept to the proponents of trans-nationalism. The basic idea of mankind's division into different cultures was not in dispute. Instead, the trans-nationalists were concerned with how to turn culture's face away from the past and towards the future.

The fundamental problem of the European experience for the trans-nationalists was how the Europeans emphasized the particularist and past-oriented dimension of culture. The European concepts of culture in both their German (Kultur), French (civilization), or British (culture) versions were to an extent competing and emphasizing different aspects of the same namely the *cultura animi* of the nation. The cultivation of the spirit of the nation included but with different emphasis the cultivation of the land and the construction of great human artifacts. The European uses of the concept of culture were, therefore, highly complex but nevertheless intimately related in their denomination of character, individual or collective, of particular habitats, and of the productive genius of the particular nation. These uses of culture had simultaneously several layers of meaning to them. To our purposes here it is worth mentioning three layers that are also highlighted by the pragmatists: 1. Classification; 2. Analysis; 3. Pedagogy. Culture was used scientifically and popularly to classify and differentiate people and cultures from each other. It was increasingly used scientifically in academic analysis in history, political and social philosophy and maybe most importantly in early anthropology. Thirdly, culture was used to describe the process of becoming something better or reaching a higher level of existence resembling the neo-humanist idea of *Bildung*. Culture was clearly both scientific and political and accordingly human, rationalist and empiricist in opposition to religious and metaphysical positions. But the European uses of culture were still primarily teleological in their orientation towards an already known cultural, national, and individual ideal. These European ideals of culture were although a future destination historical in the sense that they praised a cultural genius that had grown out of pristine pasts. This past-oriented future optimism was nowhere more explicit than in the rapidly increasing establishment of and popular interest in museums and exhibitions.

To the American, pragmatist intellectuals it was crucial that America was founded on individual and collective desires to be free from the European pasts and the social roles they set people in. The European historical idealism was reductive and particularist in the perspective of the pragmatists which led to violent integration and assimilation processes with the aim of creating homogeneous national cultures. Immigrants to America were very often the victims of these processes, although many Americans advocated strong normalizing integrations processes in America too. Kallen, Bourne, and Dewey were concerned with what they experienced as the Europeanization of American cultural politics.

It was Horace M. Kallen who delivered the most explicit exposition of how a change of the meaning of culture was essential to the development of a new cultural politics. In Kallen's perspective, a point he developed in his later cultural philosophy, culture and difference are conditions for man just as the natural world itself is full of differences. But despite these differences man shares a basic identity. Man shares so much identity that the different cultures are consequences of different lives, histories and different habitats, not historical essences (Horace M Kallen, 1956, p. 12). Kallen had already in 1909 explained pragmatism's understanding of culture indirectly in a discussion with critics of pragmatism over how to understand universalism. He argued that the universal is what can be identified as common for all men (Horace M Kallen, 1909, p. 657). This was not meant idealistically or nominally but in a pragmatic, realist manner in which universally recognizable criteria for man are both historically changeable and common sensical. They are what they appear to be. The more universals we add to characterize man, the more particular he gets and eventually we reach *a man*. A particular man is a complex universal meaning particular and universal at the same time. Kallen and the other pragmatists completely rejected historical idealism and pure reason. Culture could not, in their perspective, be defined as more than what makes people appear different and the same at the same time. Put in Percian logic, *a culture/ethnic group's particularity* is a sign that refers to an object: On the face of it, the object is *this particular group's culture* but more dynamically *culture's effects as such*. The interpretant's (a person) immediate perception of this group of people will depend on his/her knowledge/beliefs. As previously mentioned sign, object and interpretant are a relation of interdependent elements; a process of learning. Accordingly, culture can in a pragmatist perspective never be an essence or understood as a historical, idealistic development of a particular genius but only as an amalgam of universals and more or less negligible features. This realization urged Kallen and other pragmatists to undertake an educational effort to change the beliefs of the 'interpretants', of people. To the pragmatist movement this was an educational and political effort towards a truer and more scientific community which was considered unequivocally good.

Kallen invented the term cultural pluralism to pinpoint the best and most realistic way in which to consider American society but also as a concept meant to counter Israel Zangwill's popularization of the idea of America as a melting pot. Zangwill's play 'The Melting Pot' had been very popular in 1908 and it praised the gradual melting of different nations into a nation. The melting pot had in the years before World War I become the most predominant metaphor to describe American society and culture but Kallen and the pragmatists found the concept inadequate and even harmful because it denied the fact that America in reality was and is made up of many nations (Horace M Kallen, 1915). In that sense, the melting pot was not a metaphor suited for democracy. Kallen's idea of true democracy was linked not only to the rights of the individual but also the freedom of cultures. It is worth quoting Kallen at length:

> Thus "American civilization" may come to mean the perfection of the cooperative harmonies of "European civilization", the waste, the squalor, and the distress of Europe being eliminated – a multiplicity in a unity, an orchestration of mankind. As in an orchestra, every type of instrument has its specific timbre and tonality, founded in its substance and form; as every type has its appropriate theme and melody in the whole symphony, so in society each ethnic group is the natural instrument, its spirit and culture are its theme and melody, and the harmony and dissonances and discords of them all make the symphony of civilization, with this difference: a musical symphony is written before it is played; in the symphony of civilization the playing is the writing, so that there is nothing so fixed and inevitable about its progressions as in music, so that within the limits set by nature they may vary at will, and the range and variety of the harmonies may become wider and richer and more beautiful (Horace M Kallen, 1915, p. 220).

The symphony of civilization is not written in advance. In Kallen's poetic terms we might say that while many Europeans and white protestant Americans wanted to mould the natural instruments to an already written symphony of civilization, the pragmatists had realized that the playing is the writing. The freely improvising and naturally developing orchestra of cultures would create a richer music and eliminate the waste and distress of Europe.

Behind the pragmatist movements' social and political philosophy we find a cultural thinking that constituted the beginnings of a new anthropological, empiricist humanism. Classical humanism is fundamentally a doctrine that claims that there is an essence; a particular immanent idea or evolutionary goal common to man but the pragmatists developed a second order humanism based on the universality of experience and learning processes; the universality of the sign, the object and the interpretant. The cultural script or the symphony of civilization has no end, no single composer and no single director apart from freedom and a universal social hope. It is radically empirical in the sense that it recognizes the fact that people generally prefer to live among their own kind and it recognizes the fact that people are different but the same – a complex universal. The pragmatist use of the concept of culture was in many respects congruent with early anthropologists such as Boas and Benedict albeit with a radically different conception of the universality of learning processes. On the face of it, the cultural pluralism of the pragmatists sounds much like multiculturalism as it developed academically and ideologically from the 1970es onward but it is worth noticing the basic universalism of the pragmatists.

Movement

The concept of the trans-national or trans-nationalism has a significant layer apart from learning processes and culture that has to do with the social and political visions of its early proponents. The pragmatists praised the fact that all

Americans were colonizers; they were all coming from somewhere else; they were all fundamentally on the move from somewhere to higher hopes of personal and/or collective freedom. This "coming from somewhere else" was a very important theme for both the proponents of the melting pot metaphor and its adversaries. But according to the pragmatists, the melting pot philosophy sought to eradicate this core American condition by seeking to create Americans in the image of the first settlers (Kronish, 1982; Ratner, 1984). The concepts of transnationalism and cultural pluralism were meant to do something else namely facilitate a shift in emphasis from the stable, from the script or written symphony, to the moving and freely evolving relations between people. An essential learning that Kallen, Dewey and Bourne shared was that America should not repeat the disasters of Europe but offer an alternative that looked forward to the future and superseded the cultural conflicts and ethnic-national competition that lay behind. If Europe was stability and history, then America should be movement and future.

Cultural and human geographer Tim Cresswell has suggested that one of the major metaphysical shifts of the late 20th century has been the shift from a metaphysics of fixity and stability to a metaphysics of flow or movement (Cresswell, 2006). By metaphysics, Cresswell means a perspective on what is normal, natural, and thereby worth emphasizing in the study of history and culture but also, and related thereto, a perspective on what is preferable, progressive and advanced. In our research perspectives as well as in our everyday perception we perform normative speech acts that no matter how neutral they seem nevertheless bear witness to an agency that acts for or against something or passes value judgments over ways of life. Cresswell shows convincingly how a sedentarist metaphysics has been replaced by a metaphysics of movement.

Trans-nationalism as a concept and as a political tool by implication shifted emphasis from nation to *trans*; to the going across or coming from somewhere else. In the vision of the pragmatists, European nationalism was sedentarist in the meaning of stable and fixed to a place and an idealistic historical and cultural script. Sedentarism is a form of organization that has place at its center. Place is considered stable or very slowly changing and the most important place is Home which is fundamentally material in the shape of a house, a village, a region or a landscape but nevertheless deeply moral in its meaning. Material places are boxes or categories wherein we empirically find individuals, communities and societies but we also find their quality, difference and moral worth. What goes between or across these boxes, *trans* phenomena, is essentially in need of a prefix because it is out of order or in a peculiar non-category. Phenomena that do not fit in a category can be considered with different degrees of condemnation from interest in this particular curiosity or exotic appearance to outright attempts at purging ordered society for this threat against society and its values. Accordingly, in a sedentarist perspective values grow out of a rootedness to a material habitat and culture means something very close to cultivation and agriculture – it grows of the soil and needs tending to produce or increase its produce of crops.

In a sedentarist perspective, migrants, refugees, gypsies, Jews, vagrants or vagabonds pose a threat to order and they are often perceived as a symptom of a social pathology that is worth worrying about. In a nutshell, when people move more than the occasional vacation or family visit, it is because something is not in order or unnatural (Cresswell, 2006, pp. 25-56). Not only do people move because places are being destroyed but they move like animals rushing through the forest or like water after a rain shower; from an area to a line where the least net effort is necessary. As Cresswell also points out, the basic assumption is that people do not move if they can help it (Cresswell, 2006, p. 29).

In the context of the pragmatist movement, their views on culture and learning, and their advocacy for trans-nationalism such growing sedentarism in America played an important role. Social unrest, immigration and eventually the First World War were important factors in shaping an American sedentarism that in the form of organizations such as the Sons and Daughters of the Revolution concerned the pragmatists deeply. They saw American sedentarism as against the American idea and also as a betrayal of America' potential as something different than Europe that could be a hope of redemption from the distresses of Europe (R. S. Bourne & Hansen, 1977; Horace Meyer Kallen, 1919).

The pragmatist movement did not consider movement as such to be essential for the development of a trans-national or culturally plural society. But they considered a consciousness and perception of movement and process as essential to their wish for a solidarity of the second order; the playing of the instruments we have been given as part of the writing of the symphony of civilization. Flow is what we can call the root metaphor of the trans-national perspective.

Trans-Nationalism vs. Multiculturalism

The pragmatists presented in the previous had heated disagreements among each other. So far I have highlighted only the common ground between them namely the pragmatist perspective on learning, culture and the need for new domestic and global policies to avoid more devastating wars. Bourne was a radicalist who died young in 1918 but Horace M. Kallen and John Dewey developed their activities in different directions. Kallen was intensively occupied with international politics and peace planning but also invested his energy in Jewish cultural politics and education in America and Zionism. In the interwar years, Kallen managed to keep his fellow pragmatists and other progressives related to his international political activities through different progressive networks and the New School for Social Research founded in 1919 (Feuer, 1984). In these years, Bourne's concept of trans-nationalism was only used infrequently while Kallen's ideas of cultural pluralism and an international, cosmopolitan world order were widely circulated and debated as part of political arguments and campaigns against fascism, communism and war (Gould, 2001; Smith, 1985).

After the Second World War, trans-nationalism and cultural pluralism's main institution would supposedly be the United Nations but the UN's cultural philosophy deviated from the pragmatists' in several significant respects. The trans-nationalism and cultural pluralism of the UN was and is not anchored in cultural and subjective learning processes towards hopes for the future but what can be called culturalism or multiculturalism in the sense of multiple ethnocentrisms and the management of potential and existing conflicts. This distinction between trans-nationalism and multiculturalism is central for present cultural discussions but also for the historical trajectories of these related but different concepts. Culturalism or multiculturalism has its origins in early anthropology and is usually related to Franz Boas and Ruth Benedict or the so-called American tradition but has occasionally been ascribed to Randolph Bourne or Horace M. Kallen (Michaelsen, 1999, p. 8). The idea of culture that guided the pragmatist movement shares basic assumptions with early anthropology which divided people in cultures that shape their traditions, beliefs and social organizations. But where anthropology in the tradition of Boas and Benedict eventually moved on to claim that culture is an ontology that hardly can be superseded or transgressed because it is more than a sum of elements; it is the result of a unique organization and relation between elements and as such an articulated whole (Benedict, 1934, pp. 37-47). This cultural holism over-determines or over-socializes much more radically than the pragmatists' basically empirical and realist approach that just observes that people seem to like to live among their own kind; that they preserve traditions and lifestyles and that this pursuit is part of freedom and it is more democratic than assimilation into a homogeneous culture. In the pragmatist perspective, individuals are not over-determined or over-socialized by their cultures and, furthermore, cultures are different but not unique. They mostly consist of recognizable universal elements practiced in different ways and combinations. What is common for man is indeed, in the pragmatist perspective, culture but as a way of creating meaning and as a way of changing and progressing through experience and learning. Thus, trans-nationalism was at the outset based on a universalist perspective on man and culture while anthropological culturalism was based on an assumption of a fundamental and radical difference between cultures. In a sense, anthropological culturalism led to a conflation of methodological cultural relativism in the meaning of participant observation of culture in praxis with an ontological cultural relativism (Barnard, 2000). Kallen's cultural pluralism did not imply such an ontology.

In the decades after the Second World War, we saw brutal decolonization wars and equally brutal establishments of national states throughout the formerly colonized territories. These decolonization and nation building processes developed ideological and cultural frameworks of anti- and/or post-colonialism most explicitly through authors such as Frantz Fanon, Aimé Cesaire, Albert Memmi, Amilcar Cabral and others (Egholm Feldt, 2010; Goldberg, 1994, p. 400). These perspectives in many respects converged with anthropological culturalism and French post-structuralism into a radical and progressive multiculturalism from the end of the 1970es through the works of Edward W. Said, Homi Bhabha, Gayatri Spivak and many others. It must be noted that these authors are not collectively responsible for the reception and use of their works and they are indeed different but nevertheless these works and perspectives were crucial fertilizers in the multiculturalist green house that through the 1980es and 90es produced a vast multiculturalist literature and an international, multiculturalist Left.

The American pragmatists before the Second World War were also vehement anti-imperialists and anti-colonialists but their basic universalism and empiricism set their ideas of trans-nationalism and cultural pluralism in opposition to recent radical multiculturalism. As Seyla Benhabib has pointed out, multiculturalism has four foundational dogmas that are incompatible with the first meaning of trans-nationalism namely its cultural holism; its idea of an overly socialized self; its perspectivism; and lastly its distrust of the universal (Benhabib, 1999). These cornerstones of multiculturalism are all at odds with the cultural philosophy of pragmatism that was behind Bourne's concept of trans-nationalism and Kallen's concept of cultural pluralism. Most significantly, pragmatism is empiricist and realist and fundamentally a universalist theory of signs and learning processes, while the multiculturalism inspired by anthropology is highly suspicious of realist and universalist thinking.

Nevertheless, the common ground is unmistakable. There is a conceptual and historical trajectory and heritage tied to Culture deriving from the evolution of the concept and its establishment in modern humanist scholarship through the 19th century. The same came to count for culture as for the nation, as Benedict Anderson pointed out, namely that it is particularist and universalist at the same time (Anderson, 1991). Every culture is unique but all people live and act in several and they are composed of mostly the same ingredients. This is a cultural relativist perspective in the sense that cultures are relative to circumstance but are still more or less generally recognizable and people live and act relative to cultures but nevertheless share ways of relating to experience. This foundational cultural *aporia* can be taken in both a universalist or a perspectivist direction. The difference between the trans-nationals and multiculturalists is a matter of direction because the cultural relativism of both is clear. The liberal pragmatists emphasize the universal cognitive and cultural capacities of man while the multiculturalists emphasize man's embeddedness in a facticity which is particularistic but nevertheless a universal condition. The direction or will of the liberal pragmatists was towards a continuous semiosis (learning) of human renewal, peace, and tolerance where multiculturalism is concerned with the rights and persistence of, and mutual recognition *between* collectives. In that sense, there is a shared conceptual and historical heritage led in opposite directions between trans-nationalism and multiculturalism.

Trans-Nationalism and Global Cultural Complexity

Recent use of the concept of the trans-national in cultural, historical and social research begins after 1990 inspired by mainly anthropological reflections on how to study and understand people culturally and socially in the age of globalization. Anthropologists and social theorists advanced new ideas and perspectives on how to study people in a world where the importance of place and boundaries was decreasing or at least changing (Appadurai, 1996). Social and cultural processes had to be understood locally and globally at the same time leading to a cultural complexity in which we find both Nigerian *kung fu* and Manhattan *fatwa,* to paraphrase Ulf Hannerz (Hannerz, 1996, p. 1). Hannerz was indeed one of the earliest, leading and exemplary anthropological figures in the recent formulation and dissemination of concepts such as the trans-national and cultural complexity (Hannerz, 1992). The task of Hannerz and other pioneers of trans-national anthropology and social studies was to illuminate and understand new social organizations of meanings and actions in a globalized world where the nation state had become an inadequate category for the study of culture and sociality (Hannerz, 1996; Kearney, 1995).

The trans-national perspective that grows through the 1990es can more or less be taken as a specification of globalization in the sense that globalization refers to universal processes of change while the trans-national refers to specific issues or objects that go across boundaries. Globalization has a universal and impersonal character but the trans-national addresses concrete implications of globalization on people and things. Accordingly, trans-national studies are occupied with people and things that are increasingly connected across increasingly permeable national boundaries. The nation is still then a key category and trans-national processes are still anchored in one or more states or localities. Kearney states, in his review of the use of the concepts of globalization and trans-nationalism in anthropology, that: "Transnational calls attention to the cultural and political projects of nation-states as they vie for hegemony in relations with other nations, with their citizens and "aliens". This cultural-political dimension of trans-nationalism is signaled by its resonance with nationalism as a cultural and political project [..]" (Kearney, 1995, p. 548). The trans-national perspective has a connection to and/or an obligation towards a locality that the global has not in its emphasis on universal and impersonal processes (Levin, 2002). The key connection to make here is again related to culture, organizations of meaning and relations between people. In the early use of the trans-national we saw an intimate almost interchangeable relation to an idea of cultural pluralism and recently we find the trans-national to be equally related to ideas of cultural complexity. Its root metaphor is still flow in contradiction to the efforts of states to create boundaries and controlled fixity. Clearly, the counter-concepts or counter-processes to both early and recent trans-nationalism are various overlapping integration efforts that leave people in-between and/or unrecognized by powerful cultural-political projects such as both nationalization and globalization.

After 2000, Stephen Vertovec, Peter Mandaville, Stefano Allievi, Jørgen S. Nielsen and others imported the concept of trans-nationalism to the study of Islam and Muslims in Europe or 'the West' in general (Allievi & Nielsen, 2003; Mandaville, 2001; Vertovec, 2003; Vertovec & Cohen, 1999). This import did not imply any significant shifts of meaning from the ones developed by anthropologists through the 1990es though the context of Muslims in the West increasingly became a heated social and political issue in most European states. As Kearney (1995) and Levin (2002) have pointed out, trans-nationalism is committed to a locality, localities and/or people and it is also oriented towards political and ideological processes as indicated by the interchanging use of the trans-national and trans-national*ism*. In the case of the study of Muslims in the West, the studies are both interested in studying Muslims as a socio-cultural group caught in-between overlapping integration efforts (as transnational objects) and as proponents of emerging trans-nationalism or even cosmopolitanism as a worldview. In this sense, there is only a thin line between trans-national as a phenomenon or an experience and trans-nationalism as a progressive norm. There is no doubt that trans-nationalism in the study of Muslims in the West is implicitly supportive of severing the sedentarist bond between culture and place. This does not necessarily imply a separation of culture and place altogether but instead a more dynamic conception of both.

Concluding Remarks

In the fields of minority and migration studies, anthropology, history, cultural studies, and social science the concept of the trans-national or trans-nationalism has been widely used since the early 1990es invocating a re-orientation and a new understanding of the consequences of globalization on people, organizations of meaning and goods. Trans-nationalism should not be considered synonymous with multiculturalism because trans-nationalism is basically a pragmatist and liberal concept which cannot be reconciled with the fundamental principles of multiculturalism. Nevertheless, both trans-nationalism and multiculturalism are as philosophies based on a cultural relativism originating in the crystallization of a both popular and scientific concept of culture through the 19th century.

When trans-nationalism was coined during the First World War, it was imbued with a significant utopian vision of humanist hope and redemption from European historical shackles, tragedies, and pressures of assimilation into melting pots. Trans-nationalism, cultural pluralism and their proponents developed a historical anti-foundationalism rejecting historical hierarchies and concepts such as "the indigenous". People are always coming from somewhere else and have all once been colonizers. Accordingly, an important aspect of the rethinking of the relations between cultures and nations was a change of the cultural root metaphor from anchored in a place, from sedentarism, to flow and future possibilities. These meanings of the trans-national, trans-nationalism, and cultural pluralism resurfaced in the 1990es as trans-nationalism and cultural complexity through anthropological reconsiderations of cultural relations in the age of globalization. Since, the trans-national has diffused from anthropology into history, studies of Muslims in Europe and other fields without a clear separation between trans-national and trans-national*ism*.

The historical anti-foundationalism of the trans-national perspective is not the expression of a general perspectivist attitude. Based on pragmatist philosophy, the early proponents of trans-nationalism and cultural pluralism did not uphold a fact-value distinction, why they could use trans-national and trans-nationalism interchangeably, but they anyhow held that Man's learning processes are universal. The theory of signs and the perpetual semiosis originating in the philosophy of Peirce led the pragmatists to consider trans-nationalism and cultural pluralism/complexity to be truer and therefore better than European nationalism and historical foundationalism. Recent uses of trans-nationalism after 1990 do not hold science and truth as an ethical paradigm to the same extent but they nevertheless reflect value judgments very similar to the ones of the pragmatist movement in the decades around World War I. Early as well as recent uses both implicitly and explicitly support Tim Cresswell's theory of a shift from a sedentarist to a nomadic metaphysics.

References

Allievi, S., & Nielsen, J. S. (2003). *Muslim Networks and Transnational Communities in and across Europe.* Leiden: Brill.

Anderson, B. R. O. G. (1991). *Imagined Communities: Reflections on the Origin and Spread of Nationalism.* London: Verso.

Appadurai, A. (1996). *Modernity at Large: Cultural Dimensions of Globalization.* Minneapolis; London: University of Minnesota Press.

Barnard, A. (2000). *History and Theory in Anthropology.* Cambridge: Cambridge University Press.

Benedict, R. (1934). *Patterns of Culture.* Boston: Houghton Mifflin, 1989.

Benhabib, S. (1999). The Liberal Imagination and the Four Dogmas of Multiculturalism. *The Yale Journal of Criticism, 12*(2), 401-413.

Bourne, R. (1916). Trans-National America. *Atlantic Monthly 118*(July), 86-97.

Bourne, R. S., & Hansen, O. (1977). *The Radical Will: Selected Writings, 1911-1918.* New York: Urizen Books; London: Pluto Press.

Cresswell, T. (2006). *On the Move.* London: Routledge.

Dewey, J. (1999). *Democracy and Education: An Introduction to the Philosophy of Education.* New York: Free Press.

Egholm Feldt, J. (2010). Arab Mentality: Orientalism, Anti-Colonialism and the Arab Mind. In P. Durst-Andersen & E. F. Lange (Eds.), *Mentality and Thought. North, South, East and West* (pp. 119-136). Copenhagen: Copenhagen Business School Press.

Feuer, L. S. (1984). Horace M. Kallen on War and Peace. *Modern Judaism, 4*(2), 201-213.

Goldberg, D. T. (1994). *Multiculturalism: a Critical Reader.* Oxford: Blackwell.

Gould, L. L. (2001). *America in the Progressive Era, 1890-1914.* Harlow: Longman.

Hannerz, U. (1992). *Cultural Complexity.* New York: Columbia University Press.

–, (1996). *Transnational connections: Culture, People, Places.* London: Routledge.

James, W. (2007). *The Principles of Psychology.* Vol. 2. London: Cosimo Classics.

Kallen, H. M. (1909). The Affiliations of Pragmatism. *The Journal of Philosophy, Psychology and Scientific Methods, 6*(24), 655-661.

–, (1915). Democracy versus the Melting Pot. A Study of American Nationality. *The Nation, 25th of February.*

–, (1919). *The League of Nations Today and Tomorrow: A Discussion of International Organization Present and to Come.* U.S.A. Boston: Jones.

–, (1956). *Cultural Pluralism and the American Idea*. New York: University of Pennsylvania Press.
Kearney, M. (1995). The Local and the Global: The Anthropology of Globalization and Transnationalism. *Annual Review of Anthropology, 24*, 547-565.
Kronish, R. (1982). John Dewey and Horace M. Kallen on Cultural Pluralism: Their Impact on Jewish Education. *Jewish Social Studies, 44*(2), 135-148.
Levin, M. D. (2002). Flow and Place: Transnationalism in Four Cases. *Anthropologica, 44*(1), 3-12.
Mandaville, P. G. (2001). *Transnational Muslim Politics: Reimagining the Umma*. London: Routledge.
Michaelsen, S. (1999). *The Limits of Multiculturalism: Interrogating the Origins of American Anthropology*. Minneapolis; London: University of Minnesota Press.
Mounce, H. O. (2002). *The Two Pragmatisms. From Peirce to Rorty*. London; New York: Routledge.
Peirce, C. S. (1877). The Fixation of Belief. *Popular Science Monthly, 12* (November), 1-15.
Ratner, S. (1984). Horace M. Kallen and Cultural Pluralism. *Modern Judaism, 4*(2), 185-200.
Smith, P. (1985). *America Enters the World: A People's History of the Progressive Era and World War I*. New York: McGraw-Hill.
Vertovec, S. (2003). Migration and Other Modes of Transnationalism: Towards Conceptual Cross-Fertilization. *International Migration Review, 37*(3), 641-665.
Vertovec, S., & Cohen, R. (1999). *Migration, Diasporas, and Transnationalism*. Cheltenham: Edward Elgar.

Between Gaza and Here: Analytical Reflections on Modes of Identification, Minority Identity and Lived Space among Muslims in Britain and Denmark in the Course of the Gaza Conflict 2008-09

Birgitte Schepelern Johansen & Dorthe Høvids Possing

Introduction and Outline

In the academic sphere, the presence of Muslims in Europe has increasingly been framed as a *minority* issue. Thus, reference to "the Muslim minorities" in Europe is now virtually commonplace. This is due to many reasons, but one could point to the work of Edward Said as being of particular importance when accounting for the ways in which scholars conceptualise relationships between Muslims and non-Muslims. Said was among the first to have as his focal point the ways in which the "Orient" was a product of Western imagination (Said, 1978), and since then, the asymmetric and productive relationships between the Orient and Occident, East and West, Muslims and non-Muslims have often served as a matrix for the study of Muslims as a distinct group. Consequently, our research questions often presuppose Muslims to be the subordinate part of an asymmetric power relation and thus in a minority position. However, the very concept of minority is a complex and contested one, since it carries with it a range of spatial connotations that comprises issues of belonging, loyalty, power, suppression and – potentially – emancipation. The very notion of someone as being subordinated implies that they are perceived of as intrinsically linked to someone or something else, here the majority. Further, the assessment of subordination rests on the premise that this linkage between minority and majority is located within a distinct space that frames their potential for navigating towards each other; if the subordinate could "move away" then the asymmetric relation would simply cease to exist. Any assessment of subordination thus implies identification of (i) a relation and (ii) a distinct space that frames the relation.

With inspiration from theoretical work on the configuration of lived space (Lefebvre, 1991; Soja, 1996; Cresswell, 2004), we can scrutinise these spatial connotations and their implications for the way we ask analytical questions. Applying a notion of social space as being practiced, lived and inhabited, rather than simply being material or conceived, enables us not to presuppose the existence of a minority-majority relation between, for example, Muslims and non-Muslims within European, national contexts. Rather, it allows us to focus on the various identifications that are constantly produced in everyday life – practices and identifications that produce different spaces and which might, or might not, involve the experience of subordination. To illustrate these points, we will be drawing on empirical material that shows various responses among Muslims in Denmark and Britain to the 2008-09 upsurge in the Arab-Israeli conflict as it played out in Gaza.[1] Rather than forming the basis for a coherent and in-depth empirical analysis, the material provides illustrative examples of the overall theoretical point.

The underlying purpose of the article is to discuss how the concept of lived space, and thereby a focus on the practices of the people we study, enables a more critical understanding and conceptualisation of minority-majority relations. The article consists of three parts: the first part is a critical assessment of the spatiality of the minority concept and its potential normative implications. The assessment leads to the second part, which presents an approach to the study of minorities characterised by a heightened focus on the production of space and the shifting character of social relations, which will be illustrated with examples from various Muslim responses to the Gaza conflict. The third part presents our conclusion where we point to a potential convergence between scholarly conceptualisations of the marginalised subject and the academic strategies employed (identities, discourses, positions, concepts and so forth), strategies that emphasise an emancipatory, anti-conservative project in the academic work.

Part One: Space as Context – the Minority Concept in Scholarly Discourse

The Nation-state Space and the Relational Minority Concept

Different social agents use the minority concept in a variety of ways: within political discourse, in policy making, by human rights institutions and in scholarly work. Sometimes it is used to denote the mere quantitative size of a given group (that there are few of them), but most often it is also related to issues of exclusion, marginalisation and the lack of power and influence.

---

[1] The material we are drawing upon was generated as part of a Ph.D. study on young (age 18-35), well-educated Muslim women in Denmark, Britain and the US, and their use of the Internet for information retrieval, communication, and activism. The study is a part of the Alternative Spaces project hosted by Department of Cross-Cultural and Regional Studies at the University of Copenhagen. Ph.D. Fellow Dorthe Høvids Possing is conducting the study that is based on online observations and 52 face-to-face research interviews conducted in Denmark, Britain, and the US. The examples used in the present article come from interviews with 3 Danish and 9 British informants, of which two of the Danish and two of the British informants are key-informants in the Ph.D. study. The informants are all university students.

In scholarly work, such issues resonate within political and state theory (e.g., Amersfoort, 1982; Laclau & Mouffe, 1985, 1990; Jessop, 1996; Mouffe, 2000), identity theory (e.g., Billig, 1995; Hall, 1994; Baumann, 1996; Jenkins, 1997; Baumann & Gingrich, 2004; Mouffe 2005), gender and racial studies (Gleason, 1990; Butler, 1990; bell hooks, 1990), and not least various post-colonial studies (Said, 1978, 1994; Spivak, 1988; Bhabha, 1990, 1994; Hall, 1991).[2] Obviously, not all scholars exploring such issues give equal emphasis to the concept of minority, but they can nevertheless be seen to form a field of inter-related discussions of what we will term the conditions of asymmetry. In this section, we present some of the central perspectives in the field, limiting ourselves to discussing the idea of the existence of minorities as intrinsically linked to the establishment of the modern nation-state and the invention of the concept of citizenship (Gleason, 1990; Billig, 1995; Asad, 2003; Appadurai, 2006; Amireaux & Simon, 2006).[3] One scholar who has written explicitly about minorities in this framework is anthropologist Arjun Appadurai (2006). Appadurai highlights the condition that the modern nation state always rests upon a conception of the homogeneous, national ethnos as its underlying justification:

> No modern nation, however benign its political system and however eloquent its public voices may be about the virtues of tolerance, multiculturalism, and inclusion, is free of the idea that its national sovereignty is built on some sort of ethnic genius. (Appadurai, 2006, p. 3)

Taken to its logical conclusion, such a notion of an ethnic genius comprises a longing for a purified community residing within a given, delimited territory within which certain forms of diversity, be they for example ethnic, linguistic, religious or racial, become disturbing. As social psychologist Michael Billig suggests, this idea of national identity is not necessarily promoted or expressed in fully-fledged violent conflicts. National identity and cohesion are also produced and reproduced in every-day practices like, for example, the use of flags, stamps, and maps, and more broadly in language politics, educational practices and political speeches – practices that Billig has coined with the term "banal nationalism". By continuously pointing towards those who deviate, such every-day practices, however implicit, produce the norm for national identity, and modes of being included in the national space (Billig, 1995). A built-in epistemological premise, according to the

---

2   This classification of texts on our part is of course arbitrary, as the work of several of the scholars could have been placed in one or more of the other categories.

3   Obviously, examples of subordination, exclusion, othering, demonization and the like can be found throughout history. As such, the relationship between the Christian Church and various heretic movements throughout the Middle Ages, or between the earliest Christian groupings and the Romans, could be analysed as minority-majority relations. The nation state and its notions of citizenship and political participation, however, have been central factors in the very production of the concept itself for both political and scholarly use.

work of scholars like Appadurai and Billig, is that collective identity and group formation are something inherently relational; they are relational in the sense that any establishment of "a self" is dependent on "an other" from which the self is by definition differentiated – a premise widely shared by the scholars addressing the aforementioned conditions of asymmetry (e.g., Said, Laclau & Mouffe, Bhabha, Hall, Spivak, and Baumann).

While the sovereign national ethnos might be the ideal of "the nation", the modern state is, however, also characterised by ideals of political participation, civil rights and democratic representation that resonate an ideal of a diversified space comprising all its citizens (Appadurai, 2006, pp. 49). This liberal-democratic ideal for some scholars has led to the assertion that the concept of "minority" should be abandoned altogether, as it appears as an obsolete relic linked to the more extreme modes of nationalism (Amersfoort, 1982; Gleason, 1990). However, in many contexts the realisation of the civic diversity implied in the liberal ideals of the modern state paradoxically runs contrary to the idea of the national ethnos, since the very existence of the deviation serves as a constant reminder of the impossibility of a pure nation. Modern states, especially in their democratic forms, thus hold a strange inner tension that produces what Appadurai (2006) calls "… the anxiety of incompleteness" (p. 8) – a constant reminder of the impossible closure of the national space and national identity, where the national ethnos is always assigned to the position as "a majority". Consequently, the concepts of minority and majority, like those of self and other, have a reciprocal nature, because they mutually feed upon each other (Baumann & Gingrich, 2004; Laclau & Mouffe, 1985; Butler, 1990; Bhabha, 1994; Hall, 1994, 1991). Or in other words, there can be no majorities without minorities.

Issues of Subordination

Not all scholars working within a relational framework of group formation and identity focus explicitly on matters of subordination, but due to the often extensive focus on social antagonisms, it is still very often part and parcel of the productive relations that are being scrutinised. Due to the idea of an overlap between territorial, cultural and sometimes ethnic boundaries, the nation-state is often spatially configured as one of the primary producers of relations of subordination (e.g., Appadurai, 2006; Asad, 2003; Billig, 1995; Amerfoort, 1982). The scholarly work is thus often framed by reference to national boundaries and national majorities within which certain groups are marginalised in different ways: examples of such include studies of the Basques in Spain (e.g., Conversi, 2000), the Sami in Norway (e.g., Eidheim, 1971), the Muslims in Britain (e.g., Lewis, 2007) and so forth. Furthermore, a prevailing perspective in such research is that marginalised groups do not have the power to define the general norms for the space within which they live. Additionally, a central issue is how minorities are subjected to pressure in the shape of stigmatisation, discrimination, lack of access to political participation, social exclusion and the like, and how the minorities respond to this pressure through various forms of counter-pressure.

There is, of course, a logical explanation for the configuration of the national space as the space that *sine qua non* frames minority-majority relations, namely that the state through the legitimate employment of physical and legislative power defines the boundaries within which minority and majority can manoeuvre. There are thus sound reasons for an analytical focus on the nation-state space, however, there might be more to it than that: most, if not all, scholars are themselves in one way or another socialised within the world of nation-states, and this way of structuring our surroundings is thus firmly rooted in our "mental maps". Geographer Doreen Massey is among those who have proposed that the very fact that the boundaries of nation-states can be conceived of as being "natural" is a result of a hegemonic understanding of space. Massey (2005) describes how academia has taken over the idea established in modernity of a merging between space and society, and accordingly how the nation-state came to be conceptualised as the natural way of organising such societal space. According to Massey (2005), the norm remains "… an imagination of space as already divided-up, of places which are already separated and bounded" (p. 65). And this condition prevails in spite of increased scholarly engagement with various types of critical theory aiming at the deconstruction of such notions of "the natural", and widespread talk of the global, the trans-national and the trans-local.

Other Spaces: Centre, Periphery and Trans-Nationalism

In other parts of the scholarly field that examine conditions of asymmetry, scholars have focussed their attention on spaces other than the nation as the frame of relations of subordination, for example, those of centre and periphery. This is the case within the various post-colonial studies; one case of particular interest for our present discussion is the work of Edward Said. Said was among the first scholars to propose that the imaginative geographies and our representations of spaces, such as the Orient and the Occident, are embedded within colonial structures of power and subordination. The imaginative geography is produced through related sets of binaries that shape the relationship between the colonizers and the colonized as possible positions within the colonial space. Furthermore, Said's work is interesting because he strongly suggests that one way of deconstructing the binaries of imagined geography is "… a persistent crossing of boundaries that is tethered only by one's political project" (Soja, 1996, p. 139). Thus, an underlying interest in the spatial character of social relations and subordination is at the heart of Said's approach. Homi K. Bhabha (1990), to some extent resonating with the work of Said, refers to the concept of third space to describe this crossing of boundaries. Third space is the transitional space that comes into being through the experience of moving across established boundaries, and it renders possible the identification of the differences that constitute the otherwise implicit or transparent norms of social spaces. Third space always exists simultaneously alongside other spaces, and it constitutes a position from which the binaries of the colonial relationship can be identified and, perhaps more importantly, challenged. According to Bhabha, an important feature of third space is that it implies a chosen marginality of the critical subject (writer, scholar, activist etc.), and this chosen marginality forms a potential resource for the subversion of the conditions of asymmetry between centre and periphery. Or in the words of Bhabha (1990), it "… displaces the histories that constitute it, and sets up new structures of authority, new political initiatives …" (p. 211)

Another type of space that sometimes frames minority-majority relations is trans-national or trans-local space (i.e. spaces that transgress territorial boundaries). A central issue when researching trans-national or trans-local relations has been how people form social relations, loyalties, and belonging across national borders, in the course of, for example, migration. With regards to the specific issue of Muslim minorities, researchers such as Peter P. Mandaville (2001), Olivier Roy (2004) and Ghassan Hage (2009) examine how relations of power and subordination are produced trans-nationally, however in quite different ways. In his article "Hating Israel in the Field: On Ethnography and Political Emotions", Hage explores how so-called political emotions are generated by the ways in which Muslim immigrants in the West experience the Arab-Israeli conflict. Hage makes the observation that such political emotions often play a significant role in shaping the sense of belonging among Muslim immigrants in the West. Moreover, he argues that, with regard to the impact of politics on the shaping of senses of belonging among Muslim immigrants, the political emotions surrounding the Arab-Israeli conflict can be interpreted as an example of how international foreign politics and local politics should be understood simultaneously.

In his book *Globalized Islam* (2004), Roy discusses how some Muslims in a Western context experience a growing sense of isolation, marginalisation and deterritorialisation within the national context in which they live. According to Roy, they therefore seek out other contexts for expressing their identity and sense of belonging, for example through virtual communities on the Internet or through imaginations of the umma:

> The popularity of the websites is thus not connected to Islamic activism as such, but to a growing sense of de-territorialisation of a Muslim [...] educated, population, which tries to re-establish a virtual space of community, replacing the dominant socio-cultural reality that ignores or rejects their religious identity. In short, it is when religion is no longer a social given and no longer has a place in societies and its norms that you are driven to use the Internet (Roy, 2004, p. 172, authors' translation)

Thus, according to Roy, the trans-local space merely becomes a "pseudo-space", in which the oppressed Muslim minority can seek comfort, but which, in reality, is devoid of the possibility of ever subverting the minority-majority relation (pp. 173).

Quite the contrary argumentation can be found in the writing of Peter P. Mandaville. In his book *Transnational Muslim Politics. Reimagining the Umma* (2001), he asserts the trans-local and cosmopolitan orientation of many European Muslims as a genuine and potentially empowering source of identity, which challenges national norms of either-or, inside and outside:

> It is in the cosmopolitan, translocal spaces of cities such as London and Bradford that this kind of exchange is taking place. The myriad range of cultures, ideas and people that flow through these spaces produces rich sites of hybridised intellectual activity. The syncretisms and interminglings which inhabit these cities also constitute the cutting edge of critical Islam – and also, occasionally, the edge that cuts too deep. (Mandaville, 2001, p. 135)

In Mandaville's perspective the trans-local should thus not be regarded as a "pseudo-space" which is always disempowered by the dominant national space, but rather as a space that holds a transformative potential for subverting relations of subordination externally (with regards to the non-Muslim majority society) and internally (with regards to other Muslims: e.g., parents, Islamic scholars, Muslim organisations and so forth).

Spatial Metaphors and Their Implications

A common feature of the scholarly work presented here is that it is permeated with spatial metaphors describing the relations of subordination; examples of such include boundaries, closure/close, inclusion and exclusion, and centre and periphery.

One of the main consequences of the spatial conceptualisation is that it locates minorities and majorities within a distinct and common space – a location that frames their possibilities of navigating towards each other. It is within certain spaces that people are included or excluded; it is within certain spaces that boundaries are constructed; and it is within certain spaces that the exercise of power and discrimination is taking place. Such spaces are characterised by limiting the subordinates' ability to manoeuvre freely – if not, the subordinates would just "move away" from their subordinate position. Or in other words, what the subordinates at the outset are thought *not* to have is a space in which they, with regards to for example language, culture, or religion, can define the norms. This spatial conceptualisation raises a range of issues, here we will focus on two: (i) the normative implications related to the role of the scholar, and (ii) the analytical implications for the way we ask research questions.

Let us first look at the normative implications for the role of the scholar. Describing and analysing the world through metaphors of closure, pressure, boundaries and subordination in the way outlined above, tends to position the scholarly narrative in certain ways. It often becomes a, sometimes implicit, goal for the scholar to open up the closure, and to challenge, cross or dissolve the boundaries. Consequently, opening up the space in which the subordinated is "locked" often resonates within research on minorities. This might be done in different ways. It can be done through the scholar's introduction of counter-discourses – telling a narrative other than the ones given by the media, the colonizer and the majority politicians (e.g., Said, 1994; Hall, 1991; Mandaville, 2001). It can be done by the deconstruction of fixed boundaries or essentialised identities of, for example, national belonging, race and gender (Laclau & Mouffe, 1985; Butler, 1990). It can be done by pointing to the reflexive potential inherent in the crossing or dissolving of boundaries by the introduction of spaces that can function as alternatives to those within which the subordination is taking place (Bhabha, 1990, 1994; Lefebvre, 1991; Soja, 1996). Consequently, a shared feature for this work seems to be a preference for terms or prefixes like beyond, across, trans-, in-between and post-. The discourse of the scholar thus points towards potential means of emancipation for the object of study. Or in the words of geographer Edward W. Soja:

> It is political choice, the impetus of an explicit political project, that gives special attention and particular contemporary relevance to the spaces of representation, to lived space as a strategic location from which to encompass, understand, and potentially transform all spaces simultaneously. (Soja, 1996, p. 68)

One of the shared premises in the field, which constitutes the transformative potential, is the notion of contingency: that the world is produced through the ascription of meaning and that meaning always, at least in principle, could have been ascribed differently. This contingency sometimes takes the shape of enthusiasm with regards to the possibility of subverting categories, and thus fundamentally changing social reality, a point that is clearly echoed in Soja's account of the African American cultural critic and academic, bell hooks, who according to Soja has:

> ... consciously chosen to envelope and develop this *marginality*, as hooks puts it, as a space of radical openness, a context from which to build communities of resistance and renewal that cross the boundaries and double-cross the binaries of race, gender, class, and all oppressively Othering categories. (Soja, 1996, p. 84)

Even though we share the premise of contingency, we wish to raise the question of whether this kind of articulation – contingency as "a radical openness" and the celebration of marginality – overestimates the potential for social change. Rather, we would agree with Ernesto Laclau and Chantal Mouffe and point to the notion of the impossible closure of social space rather than the radical openness, as an adequate way of conceptualising the contingent character of social relations, identities, and group formations (Laclau & Mouffe, 1985, p. 111). This might be perceived as merely semantics, but it is our conviction that the two different conceptualisations tend to point in different directions with regards to the way we ask analytical questions. Hence, while the notion of a radical openness, as stated, points towards emancipation and empowerment, the notion of an impossible closure prompts a focus on the inertness that is often part of the structures of domination and subordination. The difference between the two positions (the radical openness and the impossible closure) lies in their approach to the political. Both positions more or less agree on a notion of the political as the space in which negotiations and conflicts over identities, resources, and meaning take place; it is where the configurations of the social might be changed. However, they differ on the scope and size that are assigned to this political space.[4]

This brings us to our second issue, namely the implications for the way we ask analytical questions. We have so far pointed to spatial metaphors implied in the scholarly work on conditions of asymmetry, namely that they comprise a notion of relationality between minority and majority, and the notion of a specific space that frames the relation. Our main point is that it is difficult to know *a priori* which relations and spaces are relevant in a given study. Instead of presupposing that, for example, Muslims in Britain form a minority group that is placed in a subordinate position towards a non-Muslim majority, or that "Britain" is the proper space to frame this relation, one should start by asking questions like the following: Under what conditions do people initially become part of a minority-majority relation? Under what circumstances are such relations stable, or rather shifting? If a minority-majority relation is identified, what notions of space are then evoked to frame the relation? When not subscribing to the conception of groups as being objectively demarked entities with easily identifiable interests (such as "class"), what then constitutes the common bond – the tying together of people – that is a necessary part of the configuration of someone as a "minority"? In the following section, we will point to the concept of lived space as a viable analytical approach to addressing such questions.

---

4 Obviously, there are also other differences between the position represented by Laclau & Mouffe and the position represented by researcher such as Soja and Lefebvre, for instance the emphasis they put on class and economy in the configuration of social groups and solidarity.

Part Two: Modes of Identification and Lived Space among Muslims in Britain and Denmark

In this section, by exploring some of the responses to the upsurge in the Arab-Israeli conflict in Gaza given in research interviews carried out between the 5th of January and the 12th of May 2009, we illustrate how the notion of lived space can be a fruitful analytical approach to the study of the relations that create minorities and majorities.

The upsurge in the Arab-Israeli conflict in 2008-9 was brought on by the Israeli operation "Cast Lead" that was carried through in the Gaza Strip from December 27th 2008 till January 18th 2009. The military campaign was launched with the purpose of ending the continued rocket attacks on Israeli targets from the Gaza Strip following the Israeli disengagement in 2005. During the three weeks of fighting three Israeli civilians and ten Israeli soldiers were killed. On the Palestinian side approximately 1400 people including around 300 children were killed. No firm conclusion has at the time of writing been reached as to how many of the Palestinians were actual combatants.

Lived Space

First, we will briefly discuss the concept of lived space, since a bit of clarification with regards to the way the concept is employed in the present article is needed. Within anthropology and cultural geography over the last two decades there has been an increased focus on how people *do* space, rather than simply how they *live within* space (e.g., Oakes & Price, 2008; Soja, 1996). The concepts of third space and lived space are mainly used to describe this approach, however, in slightly different ways. For example, geographer Tim Cresswell describes the concept of third space as an analytical strategy to overcome distinctions such as subjective/objective, empirical/mental, and real/imagined in the perceptions of space. The term "third" is used to mark the trialectics of spatiality: that space is at one and the same time perceived, conceived and lived (Cresswell, 2004, p. 38, see also Soja, 1996, p. 74). Thus space cannot be conceptualised as something either self-evidently given or something simply imagined; in the processes of *doing* space, it becomes more than either/or, it becomes both (Soja, 1996, p. 60). Space might be produced in social practice, but it takes on – at least momentarily – an objective existence for the people doing it.

A slightly different approach to third space is the one represented in the work of Homi K. Bhabha, where more emphasis is put on the emancipatory potential of marginality. In Bhabha's work, third space is, as mentioned in the previous section, conceptualised as a productive and transformative resource for marginalised subjects, and third space is thus "... where newness enters the world" (Bhabha, 1990; see also Soja, 1996, pp. 139). As discussed, this heightened focus on newness, transformation and liberation might be analytically problematic as it downplays the inertia of social space. Therefore, rather than over-emphasising mobility and fluidity as the leitmotif of current everyday life, we follow Cresswell and prioritise an approach to lived space that affirms the "... dialectics of fixity and flow – of place and mobility" (Cresswell & Uteng, 2008, p. 2). Since we do not employ a spatial approach that resonates with the liberating potential of "in-betweeness" in Bhabha's work, we use the term lived space rather than third space. From an analytical perspective the concept of lived space makes it possible to ask questions about who is near and who is distant in the space that is lived. Who shares the space and who contests it? How do people bring modes of being in the world into their everyday life? And, how are these positions either momentarily fixed or opened for contestation?

Between Gaza and "Here"

The Gaza conflict was not the main topic of the interviews that we are drawing upon, however, the conflict, and the various Muslim responses to it (for example, statements made by spokespersons from Muslim organisations in the mass media and political debates, or the overwhelming amount of communication that the upsurge instigated via the Internet) inevitably seemed to absorb the attention of the interviewees.[5] In the following, we do not distinguish stringently between the Danish and the British contexts. The reason for this is that although we would usually find differences between identification and ideas of belonging between the Danish and British interviewees, the upsurge in the Gaza conflict seemed, at least temporarily, to lessen some of these "usual differences". Prior to the upsurge of violence in Gaza, the Arab-Israeli conflict had also played a role in the research interviews, especially when probing about the kind of news and political issues the interviewees were interested in. But from January 2009 and onwards, a shift could be identified: the Arab-Israeli conflict was no longer something interviewees would mention as simply "a relevant current issue in the news". Instead, interviewees would talk about the conflict in an intensely emotional way, often framing their

---

5 It should be noted that the historical dimensions of the Arab-Israeli conflict (including prior upsurges in the conflict) did not seem to be something that played a role for the interviewees. Thus, even though the upsurge in the Gaza conflict absorbed the interviewees' attention, they would most often avoid getting into discussions about more specific historical or political dimensions of the Arab-Israeli conflict.

reactions as a response to what they saw as a "Western bias in favour of Israel", and such a shift can be said to illustrate the structuring and re-structuring potential of already existing space (Gaza, Israel, Britain or Denmark). The interviewees, both in a Danish and British context, would often link this bias to their evaluation of (i) the Danish, British or Western foreign policy towards Israel, and (ii) the Danish or British domestic politics and current debates on Muslim minorities – two issues that had previously been articulated quite separately. The interviewees would describe how this link between foreign policy and their current minority position had affected their notions of belonging and feeling at home in Denmark or Britain. Thus, in the autumn of 2008, interviewees would mostly position themselves within the broad category of "Muslim citizens", emphasising their citizenship within a given national space (i.e., Denmark or Britain), and thereby accentuate a nationally defined sense of belonging. As such, they would downplay, or sometimes even dismiss, a minority position, and they would often seek to align themselves with the non-Muslim majority society by describing and emphasising their activities and identity as being of "the same kind" as that of the majority. In this connection, Muslims in Muslim majority societies, and especially their official representatives, would often be casted in the role of the distant other. In the production of their space, the interviewees explicitly excluded these Muslims as old-fashioned, conservative and often undemocratic, thereby confirming themselves as part of a modern, democratic, Western society (Laclau & Mouffe, 1985, pp. 103). In their attempt to produce a coherent space (British or Danish) in which Muslims and non-Muslims align as citizens, the interviewees, however, at the same time implicitly show their awareness of inherent power structures that affect their production of space (Massey, 2005, p. 10). When participating in interviews during the upsurge in the Gaza conflict, the interviewees would more frequently position themselves as "a minority", albeit in a highly diversified manner: for example, as Muslim minorities subordinated a non-Muslim national majority; as part of a global Muslim minority subordinated Western politics; or as a minority within the "Muslim community" because of deviating opinions on how to understand and interpret the Gaza conflict. An example of such a deviating opinion expressed by some interviewees was the explicit refutation of statements like those of the Muslim Council of Britain's deputy secretary-general Daud Abdullah, who openly supported Hamas. The interviewees did not necessarily disagree with the support for Hamas as such, but they regarded the statements as strategically unwise since it gave the British government a welcomed opportunity to denounce the Muslim Council of Britain as an appropriate partner in policy making. The shift in position that we have identified (from Muslim citizen to Muslim minority) at one level points to the fluid character of social identification and group formation. At another level, however, it might also be an indication of the fragile character of the category "Muslim citizen" since the upsurge in the Gaza conflict seemed to elicit demands for loyalty from several sides, mainly a demand to identify as a Muslim minority in the world (for example from the Muslim Council of Britain) and a simultaneous demand to downplay exactly this identification (from British politicians and the media). The demands point to the inherent power relations that attempt to fixate the space in which the interviewees can navigate. When conducting interviews in Birmingham and London during the first part of January 2009, it became increasingly clear that what in late December 2008 might have presented itself as a distant and violent conflict far from Britain increasingly became a local matter. The transplant of the conflict to a local setting reconfigured the space of the interviewees in such a way that it was experienced as structured by pressure. The pressure was initiated by events taking place in Gaza, and the international reactions to these events, but the interviewees also experienced the pressure as being transmitted by national actors. It is worth noting that identification and the experience of pressure might shift several times during a relatively short period of time as can be seen in the following example. A British interviewee was formerly affiliated with a large, well-know Muslim organisation working with international humanitarian aid. She described how, when walking through her neighbourhood to go to the university in the morning, she would always meet a bunch of youngsters just hanging out in the streets without anything to do or anywhere to go. Seeing them time and time again made her think that they were in as much need of her time and help as those people she could benefit by working with the large Muslim organisation. After having given the matter weeks of thought, she ended up leaving her volunteer position in the Muslim organisation in order to put her efforts into local volunteer work with a youth group. A central point for her was that this shift had nothing to do with religious obligations, or promoting Islam (da'wa), but was driven by her desire to make a difference in her local neighbourhood. However, the youth group was based at the local mosque, and all the young people attending their activities where Muslims. During the upsurge in the Gaza conflict she again shifted attention, and re-joined the Muslim organisation in order to help "fellow Muslims in Gaza". She left the organisation again after a while, approaching instead some of the local university based inter-faith groups in order to influence their understanding of the conflict. During our conversations, she reflected upon how she had experienced pressure from fellow Muslims to feel and express solidarity with, and belonging to, a global and trans-national Muslim community – a pressure elicited by the events in Gaza, and a pressure she had not experienced when working with the youth group. More generally, it appeared that the trans-national identification among many of the interviewees was related to a heightened attention to issues of subordination, and that this challenged their notions of belonging and feeling at home. The course of events in the example above illustrates how the interviewee's perceptions of respectively close and distant others changed, and how the spaces that framed these relations fluctuated between the local streets, the university, a shared space for Muslims in Britain and Muslims in Gaza, and subsequently, a space constituted by an inter-faith based interest in the Arab-Israeli conflict.

Boundaries, and connection and loyalties within and across them, are part and parcel of understanding social relations such as the ones exemplified by the young woman mentioned above. However, rather than presupposing the existence of various boundaries that *a priori* shape identities and social relations, the concept of lived space renders possible a mode of analysis in which attention is drawn towards the spaces where the effects of differences appear, and where social relations and places are never fully established (Cresswell, 2004, pp. 38). Rather than something fully established, place is a mode of being in the world, and in order for a place to exist, people have to keep *doing* it. It is thus an oversimplification to assume young Muslims to have, for example, a Muslim minority identity, framed by the British nation-state space, or to presuppose them to have a Muslim identity linking them to a global umma. At the same time, relations of power obviously exist, and they frame, at least partly, young Muslims' possibilities of navigating.

If we return to the issue of the analytical questions that we raised as central for the study of minority-majority relations, the presented examples serve as a pertinent reminder that we have to ask (i) under what conditions do people become a part of such a relation, (ii) under what circumstances are such relations stable or shifting and (iii) what notions of space are evoked to frame these relations?

Without exception, all interviewees expressed their sympathy towards the civil victims of what was often referred to as "the Israeli aggression". Moreover, all interviewees – with varying intonation – expressed their feeling of being part of a global Muslim minority, a minority that had once again become the victim of aggression. Among the interviewees it could be observed, especially during February 2009 and the months that followed, that less and less emphasis was being placed on how the upsurge in the Gaza conflict obscured Muslim and non-Muslim relations in Denmark and Britain respectively. Instead, the interviewees would emphasise increasingly the "actual Palestinian issue", and discussions would focus on questions such as: "Will there be a Palestinian state", "Under which circumstances should Hamas be thought of as an equal political partner", and "What can my country do to put pressure on Israel?" Such discussions might reflect a re-articulation of identification as a Danish or British citizen that involves a connection between one's own interests and the state as a possible and legitimate promoter of these interests – a connection that from the perspective of the nation-state relocates the interviewees in their "proper place" as part of a Danish or British national community.

Returning to the responses of the interviewees in the beginning of 2009, they often expressed a sense of being *placed* in a minority position, or in the periphery of Danish and British public debate on issues related to the upsurge in the Gaza conflict. The position in the periphery, however, was configured in quite different ways. For example, some interviewees would say that the minority position confirmed their previous assumption that "when the topic is loyalty towards Muslims in the Middle East, we are not considered as citizens here", while others would say that the current minority position served as an incentive to stress that they were in fact "British Muslims" or "Danish Muslims". Interviewees' positions on what to do in the current situation were highly diverse, and yet they had one common denominator, namely the idea that the Gaza conflict travelled to Britain and Denmark and reconfigured the landscape of Muslim voices and organisations. Let us examine a few examples. One interviewee, affiliated with the Muslim Council of Britain, expressed her regrets that British politicians seemed to be taking advantage of the situation by distancing themselves from the Muslims who were taking their protests to the streets of major British cities. Moreover, she expressed concern that the various statements from Muslim organisations in Britain on whether Muslims should protest in the streets, or simply stay at home and pray would end up dividing "the Muslim community" and make it harder for them to gain political influence. Somewhat similar concerns were expressed by other interviewees, among them a Danish woman who pointed to some of the less fortunate effects of the Gaza conflict on relations between Danish Muslims and non-Muslims. According to her, some of the demonstrations in Copenhagen in mid-January 2009 had evolved in an undesirable manner that could easily be read into a larger narrative concerning the already problematic relations between Danish Muslims and non-Muslims. She was concerned that the carrying of dolls covered with stage-blood, the loudness of the demonstrators yelling "down, down USA" or "Allahu akbar", and the sometimes violent development of the protest demonstrations would perhaps remind the Danes of the reactions to the publication of the cartoons of the Prophet Mohammad by the Danish daily *Jyllandsposten*.[6] Thus, a "semantic stretch" potentially linking the two so far unrelated events (Gaza and the cartoon-crisis) was established, and she was concerned that this would lead to a distorted image of the Muslim community in Denmark.[7]

---

6   For a video of the demonstration she is referring to, see for example, http://politiken.tv/nyheder/indland/article628746.ece. (Accessed May 2009)

7   Our use of the notion of semantic stretch differs slightly from the one presented by G. E. R. Lloyd (2006). Lloyd uses the notion of semantic stretch to overcome a crude dichotomy between a literal and a metaphorical use of terms. We use the notion to direct attention to the ways in which people sometimes draw upon their understanding and interpretation of prior, often unrelated, events, when understanding current events. A semantic stretch can thus indicate how a current event is incorporated into "a more general situation".

With regard to the potentially shifting nature of minority-majority relations and the spaces that frame them, an interesting perspective is that, before January 2009, interviewees would most often argue that there was no such thing as "a Muslim community" in Britain or Denmark, simply because the differences among Muslims are too significant. In contrast, the current circumstances seemed to make many interviewees emphasise exactly this sense of belonging to a community: a global Muslim community *and* a national Danish or British Muslim community. An obvious conclusion could be that these responses indicate or reflect a transnational dimension of European Muslims' political identities (see also Hage 2009). However, many interviewees would underline that, rather than a general feeling, their sense of belonging to a Muslim community was strictly related to fighting *the current* injustice to Muslims only, and they would usually not consider themselves as belonging to a subordinated Muslim minority in Britain or Denmark, or globally for that matter. The current position as part of a global Muslim minority subordinated Western politics would be evaluated as ultimately caused by the state of Israel, and not by Britain or Denmark, because they, as one interviewee said, "had to express some level of support for Israel, because democratic states cannot do otherwise". Even though the event and its immediate effects might be seen as "Israel's fault", most interviewees would, as hinted at earlier, predict that the long-term effects of the event would entail internal conflicts among Muslims globally and locally. Following this prediction, some interviewees would point to the need for a more intense unification of Muslim and non-Muslim groups. Other interviewees, in both Denmark and Britain, would point to the unifying effects of the Gaza conflict, at least for a while, making the Muslim community come together. It is important to note here that by stressing the temporality of their trans-national solidarity with other Muslims, and by expressing understanding for the policy of their respective states towards Israel, the interviewees cling to the citizen category. They are thus acutely aware of the condition that this identity as a citizen is not self evidently a given for them, and that others are in a position in which they have the power to challenge this identity by excluding them from the national communality.

Part Three: Conclusions

A central question obviously remains: are the interviewees part of a European/Danish/British Muslim minority? As we hope to have shown, this question cannot be answered straightforwardly with either yes or no. Paying attention to the way the interviewees navigate shows a variety of identifications and social relations that constitute the space in different ways: such as, for example, the world, Britain, Birmingham, my neighbourhood etc. Sometimes such spaces involve the sense of being in the margin of place, of subordination, and at other times such a position as "a minority" is denied. The shifts in space and identification can be seen as an indication of the need for the scholars' ongoing assessment of whether the people studied are a minority or not. Conversely, beneath the shifts there seems to lay power structures that impose fixity on the interviewees' possibilities of movement, and this fixity points in the direction that, even when explicitly denied, the interviewees can be perceived of as affected by relations of subordination. The discussion relates to the question of whether people can be said to have agency (for example that they refuse categorisation, choose their own identity, and potentially subvert minority-majority relations) or whether they are unconsciously subjected to broader structures of power. Further, it relates the analytical prioritisation of insider and outsider perspectives: when people make an assessment that they are *not* subordinate, to what extent do we as researchers then take this assessment at face value? We will argue that answering such questions cannot simply be a matter of choosing between either the perception of Muslims as having a "super-agency" (where the researcher altogether dismisses the concept of minority as being defined by the subordinate position), or choosing the more traditional Marxist perception of the subaltern as being almost inevitably fixed in structures of dominance. Rather, we will argue that the spatial focus heightens our attention to the fact that the actual unfolding of social relations and identifications is dependent on the space that frames the relation.

The perspective presented in this article does not offer the means to simply choose between the one and the other – either they are *sometimes* a minority depending on space and relations, or they *are* a minority whether they themselves articulate and accept this or not. What we do argue is that the concept of lived space can offer analytical tools that enable a more precise and detailed assessment of the modes of identification that produce a given space – and this assessment can form the basis for informed discussions of the conditions of asymmetry.

By pointing to fluidity and fixity as both inherent in the concept of contingency, and by pointing to the notion of the impossible closure of the social space rather than its radical openness, we have also argued for cautiousness concerning the tendency to celebrate the fluidity as a means of emancipation. One of the reasons for this cautiousness is obviously that a constant focus on change and fluidity potentially makes one blind to the things that are still fixated. Another reason for cautiousness is the way this celebration shapes the marginalised or subordinated subject. The virtues that the work of, for example, Bhabha, Said, bell hooks and Soja ascribe to the marginalised subject are, as mentioned, renewal, transformation, the dissolving of fixed boundaries and essentialised identities, and the ability to see something that others cannot – all virtues that follow from the position as "in-between". These virtues curiously mirror or echo the scholarly ideals of the various social constructionist approaches and post-studies (post-colonial, post-structuralist, post-Marxist). This is potentially problematic because the scholars – in their eagerness to empower the marginalised subjects – actually represent them as incarnations of resources that they do no necessarily have (but which the scholars often have themselves). Celebrating the in-betweeness as a transformative space, in which the marginalised potentially can subvert the subordination, makes it difficult to directly address the situations in which actual discrimination, suppression and exclusion take place.

References

Amersforth, H. van (1982). *Immigration and the Formation of Minorities: The Dutch Experience 1945-1975.* Cambridge: Cambridge University Press.

Amiraux, V. & Simon, P. (2006). There are no Minorities here: Cultures of Scholarship and Public Debate on Immigrants and Integration in France. *International Journal of Comparative Sociology, vol 47 (3-4).*

Appadurai, A. (2006). *Fear of Small Numbers. A geography of Anger.* Durham and London: Duke University Press.

Asad, T. (2003). *Formations of the Secular. Christianity, Islam, Modernity.* Stanford: Stanford University Press.

Baumann, G. (1996). *Contesting Culture. Discourses of Identity in Multi-Ethnic London.* Cambridge: Cambridge University Press.

Baumann, G., & Gingrich, A. (eds.) (2004). *Grammars of Identity/Alterity. A Structural Approach.* New York: Berghahn Books.

Bhabha, H. (1990): The Third Space. In J. Rutherford (ed.), *Identity, Community, Culture, Difference.* London: Lawrence and Wishart.

–, (1994). *The Location of Culture.* London: Routledge.

Billig, M. (1995). *Banal Nationalism.* London: Sage.

Butler, J. (1990). *Gender Trouble.* New York: Routledge.

Cresswell, T. (2004). *Place. A Short Introduction.* Oxford: Blackwell.

Eidheim, H. (1971). When Ethnic Identity is a Social Stigma. In H. Eidheim, *Aspects of the Lappish Minority Situation.* Oslo: Universitetsforlaget.

Gleason, P. (1991). *Minorities* (Almost) All: The *Minority* Concept in American Social Thought. *American Quarterly 43*, pp. 392-424.

Gilroy, P. (1993). *The Black Atlantic.* Harvard: Harvard University Press.

Hage, G. (2009). Hating Israel in the Field: On Ethnography and Political Emotions. *Anthropological Theory 9*, pp. 59-79.

Hall, S. (1991). Old and New Identities, Old and New Ethnicities. In A. King (ed.), *Culture, Globalization, and the World System.* London: Macmillan.

–, (1996). Introduction: Who Needs "Identity"? In S. Hall & P. Du Gay (eds.), *Questions of Cultural Identity*. London: Sage.
Hooks, Bell (1990). *Yearning*. Boston: South End Press.
Hvenegaard-Lassen, K. (1996): *Grænseland. Minoriteter, rettigheder og den nationale idé*. Skive: Det Danske Center for Menneskerettigheder.
Jenkins, R. (1997). *Rethinking Ethnicity. Arguments and Explorations*. London: Sage.
Jessop, B. (1996). *State Theory. Putting the Capitalist State in its Place*. Cambridge: Polity Press.
Johansen, Birgitte Schepelern & Possing, Dorthe Høvids (2006). Muslimer – en minoritet i Europa? In: *Nordnytt 98/2006*. København: Museumstjenesten/Syddansk Universitetsforlag.
Lefebvre, H. (1991). *The Production of Space*. Oxford: Blackwell.
Lewis, P. (2007). *Young, British and Muslim*. London: Continuum
Mandaville, P. (2001). *Transnational Muslim Politics. Reimagining the Umma*. London: Routledge.
Massey, D. (2005). *For Space*. London: Sage.
Mouffe, C. (2005). *On the Political*. London: Routledge.
Oakes, T. & Price, P. L. (2008). *The Cultural Geography Reader*. London: Routledge.
Roy, O. (2004). *Den globaliserede islam*. København: Forlaget Vandkunsten.
Said, E. (1978). *Orientalism. Western Conception of The Orient*. London: Penguin.
–, (1994). *Den intellektuelles ansvar. Reith Forelæsningerne 1993*. København: Gyldendal.
Soja, E. W. (1996). *Thirdspace. Journeys to Los Angeles and other Real-and-imagined Places*. Oxford: Blackwell.
Spivak, G. (1988). Can the Subaltern Speak? In Nelson, C. & Grossberg, L., *Marxism and the Interpretation of Culture*. Basingstoke: Macmillan Education.
Uteng, T. P. & Cresswell, T. (eds.) (2008). *Gendered Mobilities*. Hamshire: Ashgate.
Vertovec, S. (2003). Diaspora, Transnationalism and Islam: Sites of Change and Modes of Research. In Allievi, S. & Nielsen, J.S. (eds.), *Muslim Networks and Transnational Communities in and Across Europe*. Boston: Brill

Hizb ut-Tahrir and Notions of Home

Kirstine Sinclair

> I regard UK as home now. When I was in Hizb ut-Tahrir, UK couldn't be my home (...). Home would be when the Khilafah [caliphate] would be established again. Hizb ut-Tahrir members are aliens everywhere, you hate everything and everybody.
>
> (Interview, former member of Hizb ut-Tahrir in Britain, 2009)[1]

This chapter studies the Islamist group Hizb ut-Tahrir in Denmark and Britain. Since its establishment in the Middle East in the 1950s, Hizb ut-Tahrir has demonstrated a remarkable ideological and organisational strength. It rejects democracy and understands Islam as a political ideology aiming at establishing an Islamic caliphate at the expense of existing states in the Middle East. In this chapter, I am focusing on Hizb ut-Tahrir in Denmark and Britain because both branches have proven to be successful in terms of drawing attention to their cause and attracting members and audiences to their public events. Furthermore, the British branch is responsible for editing and distributing all English language material sent out to English speaking branches which places the branch in the engine room of Hizb ut-Tahrir internationally (interview with Respondent B, 2009). An example of the success of the Danish branch would be that it now represents all of Scandinavia as signalled by the current signature: "Hizb ut-Tahrir Scandinavia".

Now, let us turn to the more specific topic of this chapter, According to the former member of Hizb ut-Tahrir in Britain quoted above, her notion of home changed when she left Hizb ut-Tahrir. As a member, she felt alienated in Britain despite the fact that she was born in Britain and had lived on the British Isles all

---

1 Interview with Respondent D, 2009. This chapter draws on interviews with six former affiliates of Hizb ut-Tahrir in Denmark and Britain which were carried out in 2008 and 2009 as well as an interview with the Danish Media Representative carried out in 2009. Of the six former affiliates there were five former members and one supporter, four men and two women. Four of these respondents I spoke to more than once. These interviews are part of the empirical data from my PhD dissertation. In total I have interviewed seven members and nine former members in Denmark and Britain in connection with the research for my dissertation. The dissertation is entitled *The Caliphate as Homeland: Hizb ut Tahrir in Denmark and Britain* and was submitted in June 2010. The content of this present chapter is part of chapter four of the dissertation.

her life. She felt as though she did not belong, and she longed for the reestablishment of the caliphate; Hizb ut-Tahrir's ideal Islamic state. However, after leaving this organisation she began thinking of Britain as home. And the British members are not alone. A former member of the Danish branch of Hizb ut-Tahrir referred to members as "stateless" (interview with respondent A, 2009). Thus, interviews with former members have shown that notions of being homeless or stateless in the world are typical for Hizb ut-Tahrir members. This should be seen in connection with Hizb ut-Tahrir's holistic ideology. Hizb ut-Tahrir sees Islam as a strategy for unifying all Muslims, and understands all borders separating states and Muslims as artificial. Often in diaspora and Islamism studies, Hizb ut-Tahrir is referred to as a transnational organisation and its members are understood to be practicing a deterritorialised version of Islam (for instance Roy, 2004; Mandaville, 2001, 2005). Certainly, Hizb ut-Tahrir is transnational in the sense that it has branches in over 40 countries, it uses modern web based means of communications (web pages, blogs, mailing lists etc) and senior members of key branches such as the British branch are sent out by the organisation to set up and assist new branches. Furthermore, the British branch is instrumental in distributing the organisation's material to English speaking branches throughout the globe (interviews with former members of the British branch, 2008-09). The academic understanding of Hizb ut-Tahrir as an organisation that is not limited by nation states and Islam as a religion without borders corresponds very well with Hizb ut-Tahrir members' own understanding. As shown in the above quotation, Hizb ut-Tahrir members feel alienated in Britain. Thus, in Hizb ut-Tahrir exists an understanding of not belonging to the West although the majority of Danish and British members are firmly rooted in their European countries so to speak. Denmark or Britain is where they were born, where they work, where their families are and often it is the only place they have ever lived. However, members are convinced that only in the future caliphate will they feel at home. Likewise, the future caliphate is the only state they recognise. Subsequently, I ask: Why are members of Hizb ut-Tahrir in Denmark and Britain more likely to feel unrooted and homeless than other people? And: How can we understand "home" and "homeland" in connection with Hizb ut-Tahrir members' activities and worldview? The answers rely on interviews with members and former members of Hizb ut-Tahrir in Denmark and Britain conducted in 2008 and 2009 and the following analysis is based partly on a social analytical approach, partly on an approach inspired by cultural geographers such as Doreen Massey and Tim Cresswell.

Against this background, the chapter analyses and discusses membership of Hizb ut-Tahrir in terms of practice and self-understanding rather than as ideology and politics. In other words, the aim is to analyse how "home" and "homeland" is perceived by members and find out how this relates to members' party related activities and worldview. Due to analyses of how members are doing place (Cresswell, 2004) and carrying out homing strategies (Winther, 2006), I argue that notions of home and belonging can be understood as both practice and ideology. Hizb ut-Tahrir members are at home in their European setting in a practical sense despite the fact that they feel alienated here. Also, the feeling of being unrooted or homeless is not necessarily a consequence of members' experiences of discrimination or the like. Rather, it stems from Hizb ut-Tahrir's ideological thinking of Muslims as victims of suppression. Furthermore, I argue that the apparent divide between ideology and practice in Hizb ut-Tahrir is by no means insurmountable. Members overcome the divide through practice. As I hope to illustrate in the following, members practice the ideology and thus the caliphate when engaging in Hizb ut-Tahrir activities.

Why Home Cannot be in the West

The core of Hizb ut-Tahrir's Islamist ideology consists of the ideas of the caliphate and of the *ummah,* the worldwide community of Muslims. Founded in Jerusalem in 1953 the organisation aims at reestablishing an Islamic caliphate in a Muslim country in the Middle East. From a historical point of view, the caliphate has been many and very different systems of rule, each one reflecting the prevailing societies and epochs. However, Hizb ut-Tahrir does not differentiate between the different caliphates and their specific characteristics. On the contrary, Hizb ut-Tahrir sees the first caliphate imposed by Arab tribes after the death of Mohammad in 632 and the last, the Ottoman caliphate centred in Istanbul (1517-1924), and all caliphates in between the two as one and the same system despite the different forms and manifestations. To Hizb ut-Tahrir the caliphate is a unifying historical, religious and political basis shared by all Muslims regardless of ethnicity, geography and orthodoxy (Taji-Farouki, 1996, pp 65-67). Moreover, with their focus on "[m]oulding people into one Ummah" (Nabhani, (1953) 1998, p 157)[2], the replacement of existing nation states with an Islamic caliphate, and their welcoming of Muslims from all geographical and ethnic backgrounds, Hizb ut-Tahrir is playing an active part in the ideological de-territorialisation of

---

2 The book *The Islamic State* (al-Dawla al.Islamiyya) was most likely written by al-Nabhani. The Arabic edition is dated "1953" but as it was published as part of a series with 7 other titles with the same date, it is most likely that these are not all first editions and that the date refers to the year of the establishment of the organisation. See Taji-Farouki (1996, p. 221) for a thorough discussion of the original Hizb ut-Tahrir material. The English version of the book is from 1998 and published by Hizb ut-Tahrir in London. See khilafah.dk for Hizb ut-Tahrir material in Arabic, Danish and English: http://www.khilafah.dk/ (last accessed 10 May 2010).

Islam.[3] The group is pointing to an understanding of Islam that is detached from the migrant generations' Muslim homelands, just as they construct transnational identities and networks. Thus, it can be argued that members are choosing the ideologically defined caliphate as "homeland" over any concrete nation state. This choice is guided by Hizb ut-Tahrir's ideologically based victimisation of Muslims. In all its 1950s ideological material and all its present day rhetoric, the organisation advocates that Muslims are victims of oppression and systematic violation carried out by the West. Today as in the year of the founding of the organisation (1953), ideologues will point at the abolishment of the last caliphate (1924) and the creation of Israel (1948) as the two main examples of how the West dominates the Middle East and Muslims. Furthermore, they will point at how present day crises and conflicts fit into this pattern of dominance, suppression, exploitation and humiliation of Muslims using the war on terror, Iraq, Afghanistan or the Gaza war as illustrative and recent examples hereof. The aim behind the emphasis on Muslims as victims is to warn members and affiliates that they are not and never will be regarded as part of the West – and to advise members that they will never and should never feel at home in a Western country. On top of the argumentation about Muslims as victims, Hizb ut-Tahrir ideologues add a focus on the moral decay and general decadence of the West. Take any issue of the *Khilafah* magazine and you will find articles on political double standards, perverted sexuality, failing family values etc. in the West.[4] In all Hizb ut-Tahrir publications and rhetoric, the dichotomy between Islam and the West plays a central role. According to this organisation, the West represents all that is evil and decadent, while Islam represents all that is good, true and pure. Thus, everything is reduced to absolute contrasts resulting in idealisation of Muslims, Islam and the caliphate and a demonisation of the West, Western states and Western ideals (democracy, secularism, capitalism, socialism or nationalism etc.). With this focus, Hizb ut-Tahrir stresses that the last thing any truth seeking, God fearing Muslim would ever want is to be associated with the West. Thus, the road is paved for the launch of the organisation's ultimate political goal: The reestablishment of the caliphate.

---

3   See Olivier Roy *Globalized Islam: The Search for a New Ummah* (Columbia University Press, 2004) for a thorough analysis of the tendencies of deterritorialisation in Islam as a minority religion. Peter Mandaville characterises similar tendencies in his *Transnational Muslim Politics. Reimagining the umma* (Routledge, 2001) and follows up on these points concerning the formation of new worldwide political forum in the book *Global Political Islam* (Routledge, 2007).

4   In Hizb ut-Tahrir material (both ideological material and other "non adopted" work and articles) the West is generally regarded as an entity, however, in country specific material, you will find specific countries and conditions described and criticised, for instance the Danish integration system.

Hizb ut-Tahrir's voluntary homelessness in the West is matched by academics characterising Hizb ut-Tahrir as transnational and deterritorialised and members as unrooted. When discussing rootedness and unrootedness in relation to analyses of transnational minority phenomena, Mandaville argues that migrants have access to a special position limited by neither physical state borders nor political boundaries (Mandaville, 2001, 2005). Furthermore, Muslims living as minorities in Western societies tend to find refuge in the idea of the ummah – i.e. a community in which the majority populations in the West have the role of 'the other' (Mandaville, 2001, p. 104). In connection with the imagined global Muslim community, Mandaville emphasises that this ideal must remain exactly an ideal and never be a 'place'. If a shared ideal or an imagined community becomes fixed in a place it would automatically be determined by the norms and regulations of that place and thereby be subordinated a majority once again. Only if minorities keep referring to elusive communities transcending national borders can they uphold an identity freed from otherness. Hizb ut-Tahrir is a perfect example of an organisation with a holistic ideology that believes firmly that its own true Islam will succeed in uniting all Muslims. Members in Denmark and Britain isolate themselves socially in little enclaves in their European homelands while identifying with an imagined global community of believers and an Islamic state out of this world. Mandaville continues his analysis by arguing that due to a preference for imagined communities, *khilafist-jihadists* – Hizb ut-Tahrir belongs to this category according to Mandaville – are more in flux than others:

> Promulgating Islam as a higher order identity, would-be-supporters are asked to deemphasise national affiliations in the name of the ummah and to understand the suffering of Muslims in other lands as their own – and as circumstances into which they are obliged by their religion to intervene. In this sense, the khilafist-jihadist agenda might be said to hold the greatest appeal for those whose sense of belonging is already in flux – those disjunct from mainstream society and somehow adrift. (Mandaville, 2005, p. 314).[5]

According to Mandaville, Hizb ut-Tahrir's European branches can be seen as likely to inspire and draw to them individuals who feel disconnected with any kind of mainstream culture (be it the mainstream culture of their European homeland or mainstream Islamic practice and interpretation); individuals who feel more detached, homeless or unrooted than the majority of people. Also, Mandaville argues that individuals belonging to any given majority, i.e. Muslims living in Muslim a country, are not in flux to the same extent as their fellow-believers in

---

5 Peter Mandaville: "Sufis and Salafis: The Political Discourse of Transnational Islam" in: Hefner (ed.) *Remaking Muslim Politics. Pluralism, Contestation, Democratization*. Princeton: Princeton University Press, page 314, 2005. In the article. Hizb ut-Tahrir is regarded a *khilafist* group due to its emphasis on the unity of the ummah, the future reestablishment of the caliphate and the categorisation of the West as "other".

minority settings in Europe. Belonging to a minority religion, European Muslims are between cultures, between countries, between homes. And because of Hizb ut-Tahrir's anti-Western ideology and their ideological longing for Muslim unity in the caliphate, individuals belonging to this group are in-between, unrooted or even uprooted *par excellence*. Mandaville contributes with perspectives of interest to the analysis of Hizb ut-Tahrir and members' notions of home as he emphasises two important points. The first one is that Hizb ut-Tahrir's ideals, the caliphate and ummah, can never be fixed geographically. The ideal state containing the Muslim community has to remain an ideal in order to remain attractive to members. It has to be something to be longed for. Any attempts to establish the state would have the consequence that Hizb ut-Tahrir's Utopia would drown in practicalities and *real politik*. The other important point supports an understanding that is prevailing amongst members of Hizb ut-Tahrir, namely that they do not belong in the West. However, after having interviewed members and former members of Hizb ut-Tahrir regarding their notions of home and belonging I would turn his argument around. Hizb ut-Tahrir does not necessarily recruit individuals who are already *in flux*. Rather, due to the ideological notions of caliphate and ummah Hizb ut-Tahrir members are taught to distance themselves from their European homelands and to think of themselves as homeless. This is done regardless of individuals' previous experiences and conditions. Some may have experienced discrimination and others may just have had vague feelings of being different or of not belonging. Hizb ut-Tahrir uses grievances on all possible levels to underline a global Muslim identity to make members work for the establishment of the caliphate. Thus, homelessness and unrootedness in Hizb ut-Tahrir is a result of ideological thinking.

Home and Homeland According to Hizb ut-Tahrir

Having established that Hizb ut-Tahrir members in Denmark and Britain are likely to feel homeless or unrooted due to their adherence to Hizb ut-Tahrir's ideology, let us now move on to the discussion of notions of home and homeland in Hizb ut-Tahrir. Hizb ut-Tahrir distinguishes between the rational arguments behind building a caliphate and the irrational sentiments connected to a homeland. In an interview conducted in 2009, Hizb ut-Tahrir's Media Representative in Denmark, Chadi Freigeh, explained the different connotations of homeland and the caliphate according to Hizb ut-Tahrir's ideology:

> The caliphate should not be perceived as a homeland, and the feelings attached to a homeland should not be attached to the caliphate. A homeland is the place one is born and raised and it is a natural instinct to have certain feelings towards the place where one grew up due to specific

experiences, a specific climate, family relations and friendships. (...) This is only natural and this is accepted in Islam. (...) But when one talks about the caliphate, one refers to the political system which is the only acceptable system according to the Islamic ideology in terms of handling Muslim affairs and implementing the Islamic system. (...) This is not based on emotional, instinctive or sentimental attachment. My attachment and my loyalty towards the Islamic state and to the political project is based on Islamic conviction and intellectual reflection. (...) Furthermore, you will find people who are born outside the caliphate, I mean, take a convert born in Denmark who loves Denmark and who loves a certain climate and certain people here and who has a lot of experiences tied to a specific birthplace. These feelings are not unislamic, but on the other hand, they have nothing to do with his affiliation with the caliphate to do either. (Interview, 2009)

This answer led me to ask if the Media Representative found it plausible that a member of Hizb ut-Tahrir could work for the reestablishment of the caliphate without any emotional or sentimental basis for this. Freigeh answered:

Emotions directed at a homeland are not rational. From a rational point of view, what is the difference between Copenhagen and Berlin? What is it that makes me love Copenhagen and not Berlin? There are buildings of stone both places. The only thing that can explain my preference for Copenhagen over Berlin is the experiences I have had in Copenhagen. (...) What is it to be Danish or German? You would not be able to find common features in peoples' answers. The answers would differ because it is highly subjective. (...) On the contrary, if you ask what it means to be secular or Muslim then you would be able to get concrete answers because secularism and Islam both have a concrete meaning and a rational definition. (Interview, 2009)

Thus, according to Hizb ut-Tahrir's line of thought, rational thinking and rational arguments is what brings someone to believe in the caliphate as a perfect state and hence work for the reestablishment of the caliphate. It is different with a homeland. The concept of homeland, according to Hizb ut-Tahrir, is inter-relational as seen in the citation above. A homeland becomes a special place to an individual due to experiences and emotional connections. Although this is thought of as irrational, Hizb ut-Tahrir still acknowledges the existence of such connections and inter-relativity. Despite the fact that Hizb ut-Tahrir does not find the West a suitable place to live for Muslims, it does accept the fact that members will have emotional ties with the countries they grew up in and live in. However, this, Hizb ut-Tahrir's official line of thought, corresponds poorly with the fact that members think of themselves as homeless or stateless in Denmark and Britain. According to former members, it seems that the situation is quite the opposite. As members they do not identify with their European homelands and that is part of what motivates them to work for the reestablishment of the caliphate. Thus, I would argue that members' engagement with Hizb ut-Tahrir activities directed at the reestablishment of the caliphate is the result of emotional as well as rational motivation.

The distinction between emotions and rationales is central in work by Liisa Malkki (1992). Malkki studies different connotations of homeland and finds that individuals may have either emotional or rational links with lost homelands depending on their social circumstances. In her 1992 article, Malkki compares two Burundi Hutu refugee groups in neighbouring Tanzania. The first group was residing in an isolated camp, the other group consisted of refugees scattered in a town area. Malkki's comparison shows how very distinct and different connotations of the homeland developed in the two groups. The refugees in the camp created a collective identity based on their "Hutuness" and they saw their homeland as something more than a geographical category. As Malkki explains: "... the collective, idealized return to the homeland is not a mere matter of travelling. The real return can come true only at the culmination of the trials and tribulations in exile" (Malkki, 1992, p. 33). Thus, the homeland becomes a moral destination rather than a physical one for the Hutu camp refugees. A destination that symbolises everything they have lost and not regained in their new and temporary setting. For the other group, the town refugees, the development was different. This group never developed a distinct collective identity. Instead they negotiated their identities individually in relation to the social context of the town they found themselves in. The result was that the lost homeland, Burundi, remained a place; a question of territory and geography, for the individuals in the town group (Malkki, 1992).[6]

Malkki's differentiation between geographical place and sentimental place is very useful with regard to Hizb ut-Tahrir. Hizb ut-Tahrir is drawing on the caliphate as both a rational political project and as something members become attached to on a sentimental and emotional level. Considering Hizb ut-Tahrir's perception of the West as other and the fact that members feel alienated here, Hizb ut-Tahrir in Denmark and Britain can be compared to Malkki's camp refugees. Hizb ut-Tahrir members distance themselves from their surrounding societies and develop a distinct collective identity. Furthermore, the strength of the organisation's political goals, the caliphate and the reunited ummah, is the elusive qualities attached to them. The comparison between the camp refugees' lost homeland and Hizb ut-Tahrir's caliphate illustrates that a lost homeland is not just a geographical destination but also a sentimental and emotional destination. In other words, I would argue that

---

6   In the article, Malkki focuses on refugees rather than immigrants. These two categories are of course very different, in that immigrants are not necessarily forced out of their original homelands or regions as refugees are, and this could influence the ability or motivation to build homes in new settings. Nevertheless, in the present chapter Malkki's concepts and points are discussed in connection with immigrants and descendants of immigrants. Also of interest, Erik Mohns's (PhD Scholar, Centre for Contemporary Middle East Studies, University of Southern Denmark) current research in Palestinian camps in Syria shows a similar pattern: Camp-dwelling Palestinian refugees and descendants of refugees in Syria are the only ones who demand a right of return and formulate this right into a political programme, whereas Palestinians who left the camps do not necessarily identify themselves as Palestinian anymore.

Hizb ut-Tahrir's caliphate can be understood as an ideal state in stark contrast to the West and as something, a destination, that is both evoking members' rational and political motivation and strong feelings of belonging. Thus the caliphate is both a rational, political project and an emotional destination. The caliphate is a diffuse homeland with rational and emotional connotations.

Practicing Home and Caliphate

In order to explain how the caliphate is established as both a political state and a subjective place that members long for, I draw on work by Cresswell. In his introduction to *Theorizing Place*, Cresswell (2002) argues that the notion of place is not necessarily bound to either authenticity and rootedness or the nomadic. Based on work by Soja and Lefebvre he introduces the concept "lived space". Lived space is to be understood as a category beyond Soja's defintions of "firstspace" and "secondspace". Firstspace refers to objective and empirical phenomena, secondspace refers to subjective and conceived phenomena. In order to avoid thinking along the obvious dichotomies, objective/subjective, real/imagined etc., lived space has been introduced as an alternative. Cresswell quotes Soja with this characterisation:

> (...) Lived Space is portrayed as multi-sided and contradictory, oppressive and liberating, passionate and routine, knowable and unknowable (...) it can be creatively imagined but obtains meaning only when practiced and fully lived. (Cresswell, 2002, p. 21).

Lived space is practiced space. With reference to Doreen Massey (2005), one could say that lived space is space turned into place in that places according to Massey consist of human relations. The key here is to analyse place in terms of verbs rather than nouns. For instance, when people "are placing" and creating homes and engaging in activities that make their lives meaningful to them this constitutes lived space.

Posing questions to former members of Hizb ut-Tahrir concerning their daily activities and homes revealed that the respondents were engaged in the same type of work and family life, reading the same newspapers, socialising with many of the same friends etc. after leaving the organisation. Thus, leaving made them realise that they had been leading "Danish and British lives" all along. Hizb ut-Tahrir and the caliphate may have been present in their homes and lives via symbols such as the black flag or the founder al-Nabhani's ideological literature, but these things would be removed easily and would not be permanent components leaving visible traces of a past political engagement. One former member explained that he had simply moved the organisation's characteristic black flag from the wall of his living room to the garage after leaving (interview with Respondent B,

2009). Another described how she had owned a framed picture consisting of a *hadith*, a record of the sayings and customs of the prophet Muhammad, on a nice background that carried a message about a group of people of special importance to the Prophet which she identified herself and other Hizb ut-Tahrir partisans with. She found herself emotionally moved by the message as a member and was proud to keep it on her wall. Nevertheless, after leaving Hizb ut-Tahrir, she had also moved house and lost trace of the picture in the move. Apart from losing the wall decoration, respondent C had altered her way of dressing after leaving Hizb ut-Tahrir. She stopped wearing the garment considered obligatory for women by Hizb ut-Tahrir, the *jilbab*, which is a long garment covering the body like a thin coat typically worn as an extra outer layer. Instead she started wearing more ordinary modest clothes such as long cardigans over jeans and shirts. The impression given by the respondents was that these aspects were not too important. The most important change was the identification with Britain as home.

Also, it became evident when discussing the caliphate with former members that the caliphate had different connotations to different people. In Hizb ut-Tahrir material, you find descriptions of a political entity, a constitution and references to a legal framework but these documents and references do not draw a complete picture of what the caliphate will be exactly or what it will be like to live there. It does not say anything about geographical location either. On the contrary, the descriptions of the caliphate are elusive enough for all members to relate to it in terms of picturing their private ideal state. Thus, one former member would describe the caliphate as a state with perfect health care and a state that had eradicated any form of hunger, poverty or social problems. Her caliphate was a state that was admired widely for its technological advancement – and a place which visiting tourists from the West envied of its obvious progress and prosperity (interview with Resepondent C, 2009). Another former member explained that the caliphate to him would be a liberal state subscribing to the most liberal interpretations of the Islamic legal system, Shari'a, as possible. He did not see liberal dressing in his caliphate, there would be no mini-skirts, but rather a state where it would not be regarded advisable to punish people and so the implementation of Shari'a would not necessarily imply the introduction of capital punishment or the chopping off of hands (interview with Respondent B, 2009). There is little doubt that the caliphate is thought of as an ideal state by members of Hizb ut-Tahrir, but descriptions given by former members show that personal preferences are prevailing when it comes to actual content, substance and details. There would be common connotations when thinking about the caliphate in broad terms, but individual members would easily create a synthesis between the party's descriptions of the caliphate and their own ideals.

Here, Winther's social analytical map can provide an illustration of how different connotations of caliphate and homeland are brought into play with daily routines, practice and places. According to Winther, creating home and feeling at home in other places than "at home" rely on mental strategies. These strategies could involve copying certain practices, for instance certain ways of unpacking a suitcase in a hotel room and arranging clothes copying patterns from home, it could involve watching TV at a specific time, or it could involve bringing pictures or books from home etc. The result of these strategies for creating home, "homing tactics" as Winther calls it, is expansion of personal territory. Not necessarily in a physical sense – one does not take over a hotel room as such – but in a mental and tactical sense. By applying homing tactics and thus doing place or living space, one can feel at home anywhere anytime (Winther, 2006, p. 190). For a member of Hizb ut-Tahrir, having the caliphate as a political ideal might collide with living in Britain or Denmark in terms of accepting life under a different political agenda and neighbours with different beliefs and norms. But it does not necessarily pose a conflict with feeling at home in one's home due to the ability of developing "homing strategies" and doing place. This point is emphasised by Freigeh's explanation of the homeland category as inter-relational. Hizb ut-Tahrir accepts that members have a special connection with the country they were born in. Below, Winther's social analytical map (Winther, 2006, p. 194) has been fitted with categories relevant for analysis of Hizb ut-Tahrir members:

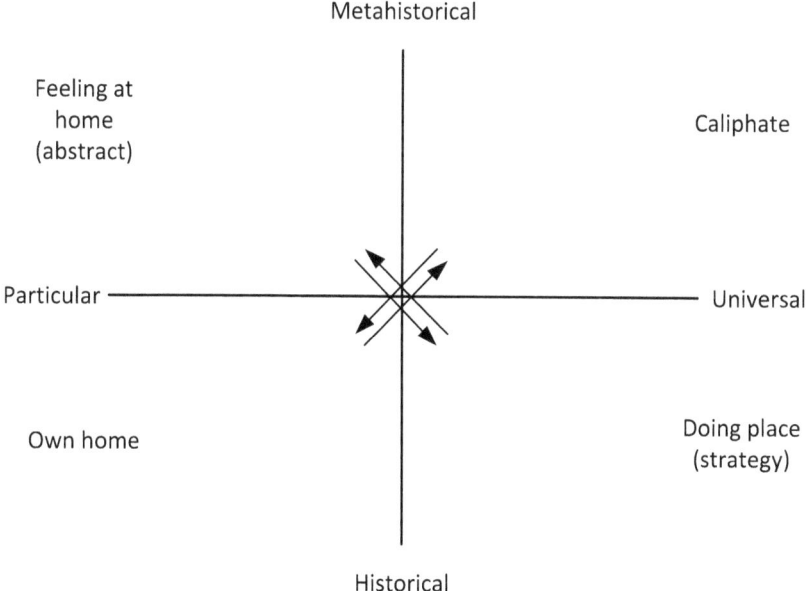

The vertical axis represents time, the horizontal axis space. The axes form two halves and four fields. Above the horizontal axis, the meta-historical categories of space and identity are found. Below the horizontal axis historical categories of place and "doing place" are found. In the field in the top left hand corner are the particular but abstract concepts of space and identity, and in the top right hand corner, their universal counterparts. "To feel at home" is an example of meta-historical, particular but abstract space and identity category. The feeling is not time specific but depends solely on an individual's ability to feel at home in a given place. An example of meta-historical, universal concepts of space and identity would be the idea of "home". This idea can be shaped by interior decoration programmes on TV, nostalgic representations of family life, or, in the case of Hizb ut-Tahrir, an ideological representation of a future ideal state.

Below the horizontal axis, the historical and thus time specific categories of place and specific place oriented tactics are found. In the bottom left hand corner, the particular place is located, and in the bottom right hand corner, specific strategies for creating home are found. "Place" indicates a specific house or home, while "doing place" indicates the strategies used by an individual in order to create home, or to make it possible to feel at home in a given place. On the map, two diagonal axes are marked, too. The diagonal axis from the top left hand corner to the bottom right hand corner is an alliance axis, whereas the diagonal axis from the top right hand corner to the bottom left hand corner is a conflict axis. If we look at the alliance axis first: "Doing place" ("homing strategies") and "to feel at home" correspond well with each other because the strategies behind "doing place" and creating home are aiming at feeling at home and vice versa, the feeling supports the strategies. Meanwhile, the other diagonal axis represents potential conflicts because it may be challenging getting the ideal home to correspond with the actual, physical place that is home. Each individual member of Hizb ut-Tahrir would operate with specific notions of home and develop matching homing strategies at the same time as believing in the Islamic caliphate as an overall ideal. A picture on the wall or a special garment could in some cases be part of the homing strategy and help provide the necessary link between the ideal home and the actual home. To sum up, the point of the map is to illustrate how individuals can easily feel at home in their own home while working towards a political goal that contradicts the fundamentals of their current homeland.

Furthermore, the map and the concept of doing place and living space contribute with an understanding of how Hizb ut-Tahrir members relate to the caliphate. The caliphate is more than an ideal overshadowing political activities – it is something that is acted and practiced itself. In interviews, it became evident that among members there was a shared understanding concerning how the organisation should be presented to the public. A former member in Britain who was involved in organising conferences and other big meetings and debates explained that female members spoke about the important "wow factor". When organising events, they aimed at perfection and tried to think about everything:

> I was in charge of the crèches and we made sure that everything was perfect – it was almost like a miniature utopia. The wow factor was important to us and we wanted everything to be like little caliphates. It had to be perfect. There would be games and we would provide lunch, water, fruit and other snacks. Also, we would register children, write their names on stickers and place them on their backs, and we would note the mothers' mobile numbers and call them if their children were crying and we couldn't comfort them ourselves. It was important that everything was organised and everyone was happy with the service. The kids loved it and would ask to be taken back by their parents. (Interview with Respondent C, 2009)

Children are known to be influential when it comes to families' consumption, so making children happy would be worthwhile in order to make parents return to Hizb ut-Tahrir gatherings. However, the explanation given about the importance of organising perfect events and thus create little caliphates emphasises my point about practice. Not only are well-organised events and hostesses with a strong sense of detail a significant part of Hizb ut-Tahrir's public staging and image as intellectual and elitist. More importantly, organising these events has had a major significance for the involved members themselves. They have been practicing the caliphate, living the caliphate, *caliphating* to use Winther's terminology, every time they have acted as representatives of Hizb ut-Tahrir and engaged in the organisation's activities. Thus, to these members, the caliphate was not solely a project of the future it was also a place they went whenever engaging in Hizb ut-Tahrir activities.

Hizb ut-Tahrir – A Complete Way of Life

Based on statements by former members about their everyday lives as members and possible shifts in their understanding of where home is or can be after leaving the organisation, one can argue that Hizb ut-Tahrir members are not lacking roots any more than other people, however, while integrated in this thinking they share an understanding of themselves as homeless in the West and thus stateless or rootless. As members, they thought of themselves as stateless, homeless, rootless or *in flux* but in actual fact, the real change after leaving the organisation had to do with the perception of Britain or Denmark rather than concrete activities. After leaving Hizb ut-Tahrir, they could think of Britain or Denmark as their home – knowing that it had been all along.

With this in mind we can return to the idea of the caliphate as both a question of geography and borders in the 1950s ideological material and a moral destination in the minds of its present day members. Hizb ut-Tahrir members link the dissociation with the West and working for the reestablishment of the caliphate.

To Hizb ut-Tahrir members, the caliphate is first, second and third space all in one. It is an objective place, a subjective place and a lived place. It is both a moral (and imaginary) destination that constitutes a foundation for a shared identity and something they practice. My argument is that this combination of idea, emotion and practice is what makes the caliphate such a powerful denominator for members. The combination of a political persuasion and practice matches Hizb ut-Tahrir's overarching holistic ideology and the practical aspects makes it possible for members to relate to the ideal. On paper, the idea of the caliphate would not be strong enough to motivate and mobilise members to work for it, but when brought into play with victim strategies and feelings of unrootedness (or voluntary uprootedness) and practice, it becomes alive and real and thus trustworthy. Subsequently, the claim made by Hizb ut-Tahrir representatives that they differentiate between emotional links to a homeland and a rational connection with the caliphate seems to work only in principle. Individual members automatically imagine the caliphate and relate to it emotionally while engaging in Hizb ut-Tahrir activities. Thus, ideologically Hizb ut-Tahrir affiliates may feel alienated and homeless everywhere in the world until the caliphate is reestablished, but in the meantime these individuals are at home wherever they live, work and engage in Hizb ut-Tahrir activities. There is no evidence for thinking that on a practical day-to-day level these individuals are not "at home" in their current, existing homelands in Europe. Hizb ut-Tahrir manages to convince members that the return of the caliphate is realistic and could happen anytime soon by wrapping up the elusive, moral destination of the caliphate in rational, political arguments and the possibility of practising the caliphate. Members of Hizb ut-Tahrir in Europe are no more *in flux* than other Europeans; they are just indoctrinated into thinking of themselves in such categories according to the Hizb ut-Tahrir ideology. Thus, unrootedness and homelessness are not ontological categories but rather ideological lenses through which the world is seen. The caliphate, then, is Hizb ut-Tahrir's answer to homelessness – it is a political project, a homeland to long for and a way of life.

References

Cresswell, Tim (2002). Introduction in *Theorizing Place*, Thamyris/Intersecting, 9, 11-32.
–, (2004). *Place – A Short Introduction*, Oxford: Blackwell Publishing
Malkki, Liisa (1992). National Geographic: The Rooting of Peoples and the Territorialization of National Identity among Scholars and Refugees. *Cultural Anthropology*, 7(1), 24-44
Mandaville, Peter (2001). *Transnational Muslim Politics. Reimagining the Umma*. London and New York: Routledge 2001.
–, (2005). Sufis and Salafis: The Political Discourse of Transnational Islam. In by Robert W. Hefner (ed.) *Remaking of Muslim Politics. Pluralism, Contestation, Democratization* (pp. 302-325). Princeton and Oxford: Princeton University Press
–, (2007). *Global Political Islam*. London and New York: Routledge
Massey, Doreen (2005). *For Space*. Los Angeles, London, New Delhi, Singapore: SAGE Publications
Nabhani, Taqiuddin (1998). *The Islamic State*. London: Al-Khilafah Publications. Downloaded from: http://www.khilafah.dk/boger/IslamicState.pdf (last accessed on the 5th of May 2009)
Roy, Olivier (1994). *The Failure of Political Islam*. Cambridge Mass.: Harvard University Press
–, (2004). *Globalized Islam: The Search for a New Ummah*. Columbia University Press
Said, Edward W.(1978). *Orientalism*. London: Penguin Books
–, (1994). *Culture and Imperialism*. London: Vintage
Sinclair, Kirstine, Torben Rugberg Rasmussen, Malene Grøndahl (2003). *Hizb ut-Tahrir i Danmark. Farlig fundamentalisme eller uskyldigt ungdomsoprør?* Aarhus: Aarhus Universitetsforlag
Taji-Farouki, Suha (1996). A Fundamental Quest. Hizb al-Tahrir and the Search for the Islamic Caliphate. London: Grey Seal
Winther, Ida (2006). *Hjemlighed – Kulturfænomenologiske studier*. Copenhagen: Danish University of Education Press

Spaces, Negotiation and Conflict: Muslim and Non-Muslim Encounters in Nørrebro, Copenhagen

Garbi Schmidt

Introduction

'Urban space', writes Rosalyn Deutsche, 'is the product of conflict' (Deutsche, 1996, p. 278). Deutsche's statement is both unsettling and appealing. On the one hand the statement is attractive due to its emphasising the impact of our 'thrown-togetherness' (Massey, 2006), particularly in metropolitan cities, regardless of this melange being a product of diverse social classes, infrastructure or understandings of 'old-comers' and newcomers. At the same time, the statement is unsettling because urban conflicts – for example, as a result of social deprivation and immobility (whether based on ethnic or class segregation or a mixture of these) – have made strong and worrying headlines in cities across Europe, including Paris and Bradford.

Although conflict is often associated with acts of confrontation, one element of conflict that, I argue, forms a backdrop to this chapter is how such social processes are linked to space, and how space inherently includes a negotiation between people occupying (e.g. living in) this space. Urban space[1] is conflictual because, through its constant negotiation, it is also political and politicized.

The relevance of such conceptualizations of urban space becomes especially obvious when describing multicultural and multiethnic neighbourhoods. The reason for this is particularly found in the politicized focus that such neighbourhoods have, included that of immigrant incorporation (Glick Schiller, 2008; Glick Schiller and Cağlar, 2009), both locally and nationally. Some metropolitan cities may boast and advertise a cosmopolitan image through, for example, glittery tourist brochures with images of happy middle-class youngsters drinking tea in front of an immigrant cafe with an immigrant grocery store in the background. In other instances, for

---

1 The conceptual framework of the chapter is informed by the ongoing discussion over the relationship between space and place in the social sciences. I define place as 'a particular form of space, one that is created through acts of naming as well as the distinctive activities and imaginings associated with particular social spaces' (Hubbard et al. 2004: 5). Place can thus be associated with multisensory elements, whether tactile or audible, and the reified understanding of what a particular space is about. Space, on the other hand, is more diffuse and plastic, involving, for example, political discourses, human interaction, relationships and power structures.

example political discourses, neighbourhoods with a large proportion of immigrants are presented as stumbling blocks for fruitful integration and a hothouse for (particularly Islamic) fundamentalism and radicalization.

Within current migration studies, there is a growing focus on cities and the variation between cities as a locus for our understanding of the role that migrants play within (mainly) Western nation states (e.g. Glick Schiller et al., 2006, p. 615; Glick Schiller, 2008; Glick Schiller and Cağlar, 2009). An example of this is Steven Vertovec's focus on super-diversity (a term pointing to the intensified variables of diversity and their impact on Western societies), which to a large extent has the multicultural city as its object (see e.g. Vertovec, 2007). Some researchers have also started investigating the importance of religious congregations for civic engagement within urban environments, underlining that religion is not necessarily a stumbling block to such engagement, but may as well be the opposite (Stepick et al., 2009)

This chapter investigates the civic engagement of immigrants of Muslim background in the Copenhagen neighbourhood of Nørrebro. Central to this investigation is scrutinizing how these individuals and groups engage in the neighbourhood, and how, through their actions, they therefore negotiate what Nørrebro is as a social and even political space. Several of the examples that I use to illustrate such negotiations are highly visual, for example, the use of centrally located streets for demonstrations and processions. However, I also try to offer examples of the negotiations that take place in much less public places (e.g. the facilities of an immigrant women's centre). As Vered Amit notes, when we describe notions of community, we often refer to extreme and exceptional cases and situations (Amit, 2010). Still, as, I would argue, Amit implicitly encourages us to do, we should also undertake studies of community making and negotiation, bridging, bonding and linking (cf. Stepick ibid.) to understand the diversity of such processes and the role that spatial configurations play within them.

My focus on concurrent expressions of how social space is negotiated (sometimes provokingly, but in other instances unnoticeably) also includes a historical perspective. Understanding the history of Nørrebro is, I argue, a necessary element for our understanding of how and why Nørrebro plays the social role that it does today. In other words, just as the current negotiation of what Nørrebro is and is not takes place in meetings, conflicts, friendships and interaction with people of various ethnic and religious backgrounds (to name the few, by no means exhaustive variables that I am concentrating on here), so concurrent spaces are created in dialogue with historical pasts. In this particular case, Nørrebro's past as a neighbourhood where anti-establishment actions often took place is important for our understanding of the statements regarding identity politics taking place in the Nørrebro of today.

The Neighbourhood of Nørrebro

Nørrebro is located close to the city centre of Copenhagen, the capital of Denmark. Most outsiders enter the neighbourhood through the main street, Nørrebrogade (Nørrebro Street), which starts from the majestic Queen Louise's Bridge (Dronning Louises Bro), built in 1887. The bridge crosses Lake Peblingesøen towards the city centre and continues into Frederikssundsvej, the street leading out of Copenhagen towards the suburbs. As a shopping street, Nørrebrogade highlights the cultural heterogeneity of the neighbourhood. Shops range from everyday grocery stores to *shawarma* restaurants, Pakistani video stores, *halal* butchers, designer fashion stores, hairdressers, and shops specializing in Muslim women's fashion. Halfway down Nørrebrogade is Assistens Kirkegård, one of central Copenhagen's oldest and best known cemeteries, where famous writers such as Søren Kierkegaard and Hans Christian Andersen are buried. Towards Nørrebrogade, Assistens Kirkegård is flanked by an old yellow brick wall. Although a historic landmark, graffiti – mainly political statements – are a permanent decoration of the wall.

On both sides of Nørrebrogade is a myriad of intersecting streets. Some of them make up clusters by referring to the names of gods in the old Nordic mythology or the names of birds. The oldest houses point back to Nørrebro's past: three- to five-storey buildings with fairly small apartments and narrow backyards with backhouses. Other parts of Nørrebro consist of houses of a far more recent date, mostly built after the redevelopment (*saneringen*) of parts of the neighbourhood from the 1970s onward. At that time the city council of Copenhagen decided that so many of the houses and apartments in Nørrebro were in such a poor condition that the only solution was to tear them down. Over the years, people living in Nørrebro reacted strongly against what they saw as an outsider, bureaucratic intrusion into their neighbourhood and way of life. The best known example of such strong reactions was the rioting around the building ground (Byggeren) in 1978-1980. Byggeren was one of the few open spaces areas in the densely inhabited centre of Nørrebro and a valuable site, used particularly used by the neighbourhood's children for leisure-time activities. By 1978 the municipality had decided that a number of new houses should be built on the site. When construction workers arrived to begin their work on 24 March 1980, they were met with a blockade by the local inhabitants. The conflict continued for another month and a half, and on 3 May 1980 the police declared a state of emergency in the neighbourhood. On 5 May, however, construction workers started laying the foundations for a new building block, and the local protestors had to give up their fight (Federspiel et al., 1997, pp. 149-150).

Throughout its history, Nørrebro has been known for its strong working-class identity and anti-authoritarian attitudes. Sometimes sentiments have spilled over into violent reactions, both the rioting around the building site and later the so-called 'BZ movement' (squatters) in the 1980s being powerful historical examples of this. In the first decade of the new millennium, violent rioting intensified again. The first of these violent riots took place in early March 2007, just after the police's evacuation of Ungdomshuset (the Youth House), an old building used by young activists representing extreme leftist and alternative subcultures. In 2001 the municipality, as the legal owner of the house, sold it to the new Christian religious movement, Faderhuset (the Father House). After the police evacuation the young people – some of whom were living in the house – were put out on the street. The evacuation resulted in several days of fighting between the users of Ungdomshuset, sympathy groups, and the police. Cars and containers were set on fire, and shops were looted and damaged. Less than twelve months later a new wave of destruction and fighting shook the neighbourhood. This time riots broke out as a result of what one group of second-generation immigrants later claimed was the police's persistent neglect of their civil rights ("Erklæring: Sandheden bag urolighederne", 2008). Since 2008 Nørrebro has witnessed intense armed fighting between gangs of immigrant of Middle Eastern backgrounds and supporters of biker gangs. Denmark is known for its very restrictive weapons laws, but developments since 2008 have shown the impact of an illegal weapons market and the increasing ease with which weapons are used by criminals, a trend hitherto unknown in Danish society.

Nørrebro, however, is known for much more than just rioting and violence. The neighbourhood is characterized by the firm confidence of many of its residents in their identity as 'Nørrebroer' (a person from Nørrebro), an identity associated with anti-authoritarian attitudes. Among people living in Nørrebro there is a deep-rooted scepticism of the police and the municipal and state authorities. At the same time Nørrebro is historically known as somewhere that adapts remarkably easily and absorbs people of diverse ethnic and social backgrounds, a place hosting a striking diversity of inhabitants. Two centuries back, Nørrebro absorbed and accommodated newcomers to the capital, most of them unskilled and poor labourers from the countryside. Nørrebro is one of the few places in Denmark which has a Jewish cemetery, established as long ago as 1693 (Algren, 1999). Today Nørrebro boasts another kind of diversity, rooted in its inhabitants' ethnic backgrounds, leftist political views, or social class. The working class still stands strong, but families with solid incomes and academic backgrounds have also settled in the neighbourhood. Parts of Nørrebro (especially around Sankt Hans Torv or St. Hans' Square) are known for its trendy cafés and designer shops, attracting both people living elsewhere in the city and tourists. Thus, Nørrebro highlights a paradoxical blur of contrasting identities (ethnicity- and class-based), violent conflict, and a shared pride in belonging to the neighbourhood.

Nørrebro as a Fieldwork Site

Understanding the history of Nørrebro is vital for understanding the events I present in this section, some of which share the activist and (identity-) political *habitus* embedded in a not too distant past (cf. Bourdieu and Wacquant, 1992). The importance of including a historical perspective on events that are taking place in Nørrebro in the 21st century became apparent during my fieldwork in the neighbourhood, an endeavour that started in 2007 and has been going on ever since. The aim of my research in Nørrebro is to investigate how Muslim and non-Muslim organizations work together, but also how Muslim groups use the public and semi-public spaces of the neighbourhood to advocate aspects of their identity. Included in this perspective is also how the actions that people of either Muslim or non-Muslim background perform with or against each other are affected by national debates over multicultural coexistence in ethnically diverse neighbourhoods, social cohesion and Islam. My description of such subjects is based on traditional anthropological fieldwork methods such as participant observation and qualitative interviews with central actors in Muslim and neighbourhood organizations.

Publicizing Space and Grounded Politics

In her book *For Space*, Doreen Massey stresses that space as such entails relationality. 'What is always at issue', she writes, 'is the *content*, not the spatial form, of the relation through which space is constructed' (Massey, 2006, p. 101). In this section of the chapter I describe two events that, each in their own way, show how the relationality of the spaces and places that people move in and out of are used actively to make identity political statements. Manifestations of identity politics are in this instance neither institutionalized or organized, but rather include public, strategic performances, including the accentuating of symbols, human bodies, and – as already noted – the occupying (and thus transformation) of physical space. When identity politics is activated, the performance often builds on essentialist understandings of identity, which is also why Mary Bernstein uses the concept of identity *deployment*, since 'identities are deployed strategically as a form of collective action to change institutions; to transform mainstream culture, its categories, and values, and perhaps by extension its policies and structures; to transform participants; or simply to educate legislators and the public' (Bernstein, 1997). We can also call such identity political manifestations expressions of *grounded politics*, statements of politics that people undertake in and through their everyday lives, including extra-institutional negotiations of identity and space through the deployment of exactly these two elements.

Once a year, on the tenth day of the Islamic month of Muharram, a procession of several hundred, if not over a thousand Shi'a Muslims walk from *Israel's Plads* over Dronning Louises Bro, all the way along the straight Nørrebrogade, to the Shi'ite Imam Ali mosque. The procession honours the Shi'a festival of Ashura, commemorating the martyrdom of the Prophet Muhammad's grandson Hussain. Approximately 3000 people participate in the procession each year (see e.g. Danske muslimer.., 2009).

Participants in the procession walk for more than two and a half hours. During that time cars and buses have limited access to Nørrebrogade and bicycles must slow down, even on the bicycle paths. The procession is headed by two large police motorbikes, moving at the same slow pace as the pedestrians. Although the procession is of considerable size, and although loud exclamations from the participants such as *'ya Hussain'* (O, Hussain) and *'kul ul-yawm al-Ashura'* (every day is Ashura) are part of the community ritual, there is a remarkably relaxed atmosphere among the many spectators who witness it. Those of my informants who participate in the procession state that the spectators are generally accepting and curious. In 2007, for example, two of my informants reported that many people politely asked them whether the procession was in honour of the former Iraqi dictator Saddam Hussain, who had been executed a few weeks earlier. During my own observations I have not noticed expressions of direct hostility among the spectators, although some may express modest disapproval at, for example, the sight of the women walking behind the men in the procession. Interestingly, in the few cases during my observations where I have witnessed people express broader disapproval of the procession, they have been of Middle Eastern background. One theory may be that the disapproval reflects the centuries-old conflict between Shi'a and Sunni Muslims in the local Danish context.

The Shi'a community is not the only group to use the central, public space of Nørrebrogade to express community identity and ideas: another example took place on 15 February 2008 in a demonstration organized by the controversial Islamist movement Hizb ut-Tahrir[2] as a reaction to what (at least in Denmark) is known as the Second Cartoon Crisis. The crisis erupted after three men were arrested on allegations that they were planning to kill the cartoonist Kurt Westergaard, one of the best known cartoonists behind the twelve cartoon drawings published in the daily *Jyllandsposten* in September 2005. The arrest of the three men once again stirred up debate and tensions between Muslim and non-Muslim groups in

---

2   Hizb ut-Tahrir (literally Liberation Party) is a global, Islamic organization fighting for the reestablishment of the Caliphate. The organization is known for its anti-Western rhetoric, for example, encouraging its followers not to participate in secular elections and secular political processes. Hizb ut-Tahrir is subject to analysis in chapter three of this volume.

Denmark. One consequence of the crisis was that seventeen Danish newspapers published the twelve cartoons that, less than a year and a half earlier, had stirred up global outrage and hatred against Denmark. Within Nørrebro, the strongest public reaction to the reprinting of the cartoons was Hizb ut-Tahrir's demonstration.

The demonstration took place around two weeks after that year's Ashura procession. At first sight, the two events shared many similarities: they took place in the same local area, the same street, and even in the same month of that year. Both manifestations included strategies aimed at creating a high level of attention, for example, with the participants waving large banners carrying slogans in both Arabic and Danish, and by participants' shouting slogans. During both events supporters distributed pamphlets and even books to bystanders. During both events too, men and women walked in strictly separated sections. However, the two events were received very differently by bystanders. The Hizb ut-Tahrir demonstration, for instance, was followed by several photographers and even characterized by a noticeable degree of tension between the participants and people watching the demonstration from the pavements. For example, as the Hizb ut-Tahrir demonstration moved from Nørrebrogade towards Skt. Hans Torv, a middle-aged woman standing next to me pretended to throw a packet of apples towards the demonstrators. A Somali man (one of the people distributing books) stopped in front of her, asking her what she was up to. The woman did not answer. Some minutes later, when the demonstration stopped at Skt. Hans Torv and some of Hizb ut-Tahrir's Danish leaders started a series of animated speeches, a couple of boys riding by on their bicycles laughed loudly and mockingly when the voice of one of the speakers broke down in the cold of the afternoon.

Both the Ashura procession and the Hizb ut-Tahrir demonstration underline the relationality that exists in and through space, a factor that is actually a motivating force behind both events. Both the procession and the demonstration are public manifestations of identity (and identity politics), and they thrive on gaining the attention of bystanders, regardless of their sympathy or lack of sympathy with the message.

As public manifestations, rituals such as the Ashura procession and demonstrations such as Hizb ut-Tahrir's are hyper-visual examples of how space is negotiated. In both instances one aspect of social factuality is that the Muslim communities of Nørrebro show that they themselves belong to the neighbourhood, and that Nørrebro belongs to them. Doreen Massey talks about space as 'coexisting heterogeneity' (Massey, 2006, p. 9), an aspect that the public manifestations presented in this paper underline and advocate, either by stressing the fact of being a minority, pleading for recognition, or else by presenting oneself as misunderstood, downtrodden and persecuted. Interestingly, both events illustrate that, when people refer to themselves as "pieces" in the puzzle of 'coexisting heterogeneity', they are not always applauded by others in their surroundings. Both during the Ashura procession and the Hizb u-Tahrir demonstration, some bystanders do their best to challenge what is going on. Reactions are most outspoken and visible during the Hizb ut-Tahrir demonstration, less so during the Ashura procession. During the later event, reactions mainly come from other Muslims who see Shi'ism as a distorted version of Islam, and who want to make their opinion known among non-Muslim bystanders. Reactions are thus a means to present what those reacting understand as a 'better' and more 'correct' form of Islam to members of the majority population. In the case of the Hizb ut-Tahrir demonstration, reactions mainly come from members of the majority, thus emphasizing that these people see the demonstration as challenging existing power relations. In both cases space is created through multiple trajectories (thus being indisputably heterogeneous), which means that the participants and bystanders sometimes submit to, sometimes challenge, the power relations that exist between, in this case, a minority and the majority.

As the two examples illustrate, the heterogeneity of space includes political dimensions. Referring to Laclau, Massey defines the field of the political as 'The moment of antagonism where the undecidable nature of the alternatives and their resolution through power relations become fully visible' (Massey, 2006, p. 151, after Laclau, 1990, p. 35). The aspect of the undecidable outcome of social actions, and how they affect the people (voluntarily or otherwise) involved and the places where they take place, are precisely dimensions of both examples, and can, for example, explain some of the bystanders' reactions. Will Shi'a Muslims, through the Ashura procession, succeed in changing ideas of what Islam stands for that can affect the role that Sunni Muslims play in the neighbourhood? Will the Hizb ut-Tahrir demonstration increase radical tensions between the majority and immigrant minorities?

Establishing Shared Spaces

The Ashura procession and the Hizb ut-Tahrir demonstration are two hyper-visual examples of how Muslim communities in Nørrebro use and negotiate the space they live in. However, whereas the identity or grounded political statements of these two events involved minority agents using public spaces to make their arguments heard, the following two events are examples in which majority citizens must actively choose to participate, and where the minority thus takes the far from uncomplicated role of host, a title that manifests authority over and the ownership of space (e.g. a home, a house, an institution). As we shall see, the constellation of minority identity and the role of host are far from uncomplicated and in some instances and to some members of the majority provocatively powerful.

Wakf: An Islamic institution inviting its neighbours inside

The Muslim Faith Society, also known as Wakf, is located on the outskirts of Nørrebro. Its centre facilitates several activities, the more prominent of which are daily and Friday prayers, study circles and the work of a very active youth chapter known as MUNIDA (an acronym standing for *Muslimsk UNgdom I DAnmark* or Muslim Youth in Denmark). Besides these inward activities, the centre also seeks to engage neighbours and others by inviting them to an Open House event in the month of June every year. The event is well attended, often drawing an audience of a couple of hundred people, mainly of majority and non-Muslim background.

The 'Open House' event has followed the same pattern over the years: when visitors arrive at the mosque, they are greeted by a couple of young people sitting at an 'information table' located at the entrance to the yard. All guests receive a timetable with the title of the talks that will be given in the mosque that day and an evaluation scheme. Within the yard people can visit a number of booths before they start on a guided tour through the mosque. All the booths introduce a different theme: in one booth you can ask questions about Islam, in another you can have your hands decorated with henna and your name written in Arabic letters, and in a third children can play games and win small prizes. The tour starts in the men's prayer hall (*masalah*) and then continues to the mosque's second building, where people visit the women's prayer room on the third floor. On the way the guides encourage people to ask questions, an opportunity that many visitors take advantage of. The tour's third stop is the library, where the visitors listen to a talk on Islam by one of the young people engaged in MUNIDA. The titles of the talk, and who is in charge of them, change over the day. Talks in previous years have included perspectives on Islam and women, and Islam and science, to give a few examples. The presentation is followed by a question and answer session. The discussion between the presenter and audience is frequently lively, and just as frequently tense.

The confrontational atmosphere is illustrated by the following two examples from question and answer sessions following talks in 2005 and 2008 (see also Schmidt, 2007). In the first instance the Q&A followed a talk on Islam and marriage. The speaker was a sixteen-year-old girl who, with great dedication, advocated the blessings of the Islamic marriage to a very critical audience. If people just followed the Islamic principles of marriage, she said, the marriage simply could not fail. Even among native Danes there were examples of arranged marriages – the marriage between Crown Prince Frederik and Crown Princess Mary could be seen as such a marriage. Before getting married, the couple had to ask the Queen's permission.

The audience reacted strongly to the speech. One woman, clearly irritated, stated that a woman that young was unqualified to say anything about what it meant to be married. The woman could not accept any comparison between arranged marriages and the marriage of the Crown Prince and Princess. A young male member of MUNIDA, sitting in the audience, tried to calm the woman down, but with little success. When he asked for the female visitor's name, she bluntly refused to answer him. The discussion continued for some minutes, after which the visitors left the room. The young woman was clearly shaken by the harsh reactions of the audience. The Open House event had been her debut as a speaker.

Two years later another woman stood in front of another audience in Wakf's library. This time the Open House speech focused on the question, 'What is Islam?' The speaker was one of MUNIDA's most experienced activists and speakers, a daughter of the deceased imam, Abu Laban. The second question in the Q&A session dealt with gender equality. Why, one woman asked, did men and women pray separately in the mosque? 'There is no difference between men and women,' a young male member of MUNIDA replied. 'The carpet that men and women pray on is the same. Both men and women pray, although they do not pray together. I think that women are beautiful, but to keep my concentration while praying I'd rather pray among ugly men ....'

- 'But don't Muslim women inherit less than Muslim men?'
- 'This has something to do with the duty that Muslim men have to support their women', the female speaker answered promptly. 'Denmark is a welfare society, but there are many other societies who do not provide that kind of safety net.'
- But we are *here*!!' the woman in the audience said, visibly annoyed.
  The male member of MUNIDA took up the theme again. 'In many other countries of the world there is a different social order. In Islam the woman is allowed to work, while the man is obliged to ....'
- This is nonsense!!' someone in the audience interrupted.

The discussion shifted on to other issues, but the tension was still there. When people were leaving the room to proceed to the buffet served in the mosque's cafeteria, one woman raised her voice when passing the young man who had supported the female speaker during the Q&A session. 'We are afraid of you!' she said in a high-pitched voice. 'Your goal is to attain a majority in this society so you can change democracy. We are afraid of you ...!'

Although confrontation appears to be the order of the day, Wakf's Open House day has over the years succeeded in reaching one of its stated goals: to attract many non-Muslim neighbours to the mosque and to show what people active in the mosque (not least MUNIDA) see as a positive and genuine image of Islam. According to those of my respondents who are active in MUNIDA, achieving these goals gives them a reason to repeat the event year after year.

Although MUNIDA seeks to spread the message through other channels, none are as successful as the Open House event.

One example of an unsuccessful event – at least in terms of the number of people showing up – was a talk held at Nørrebro library in the summer of 2007. The library had decided to focus on Islam as part of the cultural quilt of Nørrebro, both through an exhibition and talks organized by Muslim organizations in the area. On that evening a member of MUNIDA focused her talk on the status of women in Islam. Several members of the youth organization were present. Some of them had brought coffee, tea and biscuits, which they offered at a table placed behind the seating. Given the many preparations, people were unmistakably disappointed when I turned out to be the only non-Muslim present at 7 pm, the time when the talk was expected to begin. Especially the young female speaker expressed her discontent with the situation: she had spent a lot of time preparing the talk, and since she was having an examination the day afterwards, she would rather have spent the evening preparing for her exam than talking to an audience of people who already knew what she wanted to say.

The two examples are useful illustrations of the relationality that public space includes and the dimensions of power that these relations include and express through space. Both events are example of how a Muslim organization in Nørrebro seeks to stress and advocate a positive relationship with the neighbourhood. In doing so, Wakf uses both public spaces (the library) and the space of the mosque as a platform for interaction with its non-Muslim neighbours. During the open house event, the mosque opens its doors, allowing people into most of the rooms of its facility, generously serving food and allowing people to ask questions freely. While I find it useful to analyse Wakf's and MUNIDA's priorities in a spatial perspective, I also find it useful to use the same perspective to scrutinize the reactions of their guests during the Open House event. What I have always pondered when doing fieldwork during these events is why some visitors have reacted in ways that are quite incompatible with how one would behave according to the general norms of conduct for a guest. The examples I have presented describe what people said, but the medium of text cannot illustrate the physical postures that some visitors used to express blunt discontent, fear and anger. Unfortunately, my fieldwork at the Open House events did not included interviews with any of these people. My data are restricted to their verbal and physical expressions. But in seeking to understand these, I argue that my theoretical backdrop – the relationality of space – is useful. What people do in these situations can be seen as a means to counter how a certain space is used, to oppose the people who are in charge of this space, and in that sense to take back space.

The visible, audible, obvious discontent that an audience manifests can shift the power balance between listener and listened-to, as well as the power balance within a certain space (also Lincoln, 1994). Further, as the Open House event illustrates, space in itself is an important factor in the distribution of power between groups of social actors. The space that Wakf owns grants people associated with the mosque certain rights, for example, in terms of deciding what activities take place there. However, authority within this space also has its cracks, as outsiders can actually oppose the representations that space in Wakf entails. The power of a majority society vis-à-vis a religious minority is a prominent dimension of this relationship.

Fighting for Space

Most of the people whom I interviewed during my fieldwork in Nørrebro were happy living there. Many described the ease with which they could move through the neighbourhood because of the overall acceptance of diversity among the neighbourhood's inhabitants. Especially some of the women donning the *hijab* said they were comfortable moving around Nørrebro because no one would mock or seek to provoke them due to their choice of dress. However, some of my respondents pointed to other dimensions of the neighbourhood that they found less attractive. One woman, Sulaima, a Shi'ite Muslim, told me the following:

> In Nørrebro there are many Muslims and immigrants. My impression is that there is more conflict among Muslims than between Muslims and Danes .... For example, when we have our [Ashura] procession, we do not hear many comments from Danish people, but we hear a lot from the Sunnis. They think that Shi'ite Muslims believe in something wrong. They think that we are unbelievers .... When I go to their meetings and ask them questions and they find out that I am Shi'a, they refuse to answer .... I know someone who went praying in a Sunni mosque who was kicked out and beaten. You feel this conflict [between Shi'a and Sunni] a lot in Nørrebro. You feel it a lot in the shops, and I hear a lot about it from my father, who has a large network.

Sulaima's story exemplifies another important element of negotiations of space in Nørrebro: whereas such acts are indeed often a product of majority and minority encounters (in this chapter exemplified by reference to religion), they are also frequently a consequence of apparent in-group cleavages and struggles for power. People may on the one hand claim a collective identity as, for example, Muslims, but sharing this commonality also potentially accentuates and creates fragmentation, as Merete, the (non-Muslim) leader of the local immigrant women's centre, expressed it. The centre offers vulnerable immigrant women the opportunity to meet and cook food together, and staff members generously offer advice on financial, legal and family issues. Merete explains:

> What unites the women is that they are Muslims .... They pray in the living room. But praying where they do creates problems. The stereo is standing in the living room, and the Iranian women want to listen to music, they do not make *salat* [ritual prayer]. They just think that

they are one variation of Muslims – they do not wear the veil. There is a fight in terms of who are the right Muslims. The Iranian women feel excluded – they cannot sit on the good sofa and listen to music. They see this place as a place where they can party and dance. It is a very sensual dance, and the Somali women have trouble with it. Especially in the room where they pray. Lately we had an incident where a Somali woman turned the music down, and right away an Iranian woman started yelling at her ... actually, the Somali woman just wanted to hear what another woman was telling her. They almost started fighting. It's a conflict rooted in being strangers to each other. But here this estrangement is expressed in religious terms, in who has the right to call herself a Muslim.

Immigrant women coming to the centre shared Merete's impression that Islam was both a symbol of identification and a marker of conflict in the centre. During my visits to the centre I frequently spoke with Maya, a middle-aged Iranian woman. Maya described herself as secular and did not, for example, wear the Islamic headscarf. At one point, when we were sitting by the large dinner table that acted as the central arena for much of the interaction in the centre (eating, chatting, doing homework), Maya started talking about the fights over religion that were a part of the daily life of the centre. Maya bluntly described her annoyance (although other women were present) with the norms and dress code that she felt that some of the *hijab*-wearing women had imposed on her. She did not want to wear the *hijab*, and she did not like their constant reference to religion when arguing for this or that within the centre. And more than anything else, she resented the women's expectations that activities within the centre (e.g. playing music on the stereo) should be subject to religious restrictions.

The two examples (Shi'a vs. Sunni, and religiously dedicated vs. secular) underline how central religious identity is for negotiations of space beyond those of minority–majority encounters. Within the group of people in Nørrebro who see themselves as Muslims (or are, involuntary to some, described so by outsiders), there is an ongoing discussion over what this identity implies. Interestingly, while only few of my Muslim informants reported that religion was a problem in their encounters with majority peers and neighbours in Nørrebro and actually described the neighbourhood as a safe haven due to the welcome it gave to ethnic and cultural diversity, several of them described intra-ethnic and intra-religious conflicts as a problem. Sulaima, Merete (a non-Muslim) and Maya were among those who expressed the most concrete aspects of the conflict. Other informants were less direct in their formulations and simply mentioned the conflict as existing.

The spaces that Sulaima, Merete and Maya describe as conflict zones for contrasting understandings of identity all transgress the boundary between public and private. Of the three women, Sulaima refers most directly to conflicts that take place at street level. Nørrebro is known for its many Middle Eastern grocery shops, many of which stay open beyond the standard opening hours that Danish-owned shops in the area follow. The grocery shops are thus visible and powerful features of the neighbourhood. Although Sulaima is not describing violence and fighting between Sunni and Shi'a as taking place within the shops, she describes a feeling of uncertainty and discomfort when visiting Sunni shops. She feels out of place within a place that is otherwise home.

Merete's and Maya's descriptions point to the more private aspects of intra-religious conflicts and the role that space plays within them. The Nørrebro centre for immigrant women is open to all women who find its services relevant, but it is characterized by activities that usually take place in private homes. One recurring activity of the centre is women cooking and eating together. The centre also has a sewing room where the women can design and sew their own clothes or clothes for their children. Interestingly, there is a significant spatial separation between the rooms where external activities take place (e.g. handling the women's encounters with the municipality and immigration) and the rooms where the women can engage in homely activities and where the interaction is more relaxed. The two rooms where Merete and her staff take care of the bureaucratic and administrative aspects of the centre are those located closest to the front door. The more private and social activities of the centre all take place in rooms further away from the front door.

While the two examples described in this chapter show that conflicts based on culture and religion are just as much in-group as they are out-group phenomena, they also underline another relevant aspect for discussions of the cultural heterogeneity of urban spaces: the nexus between the private and public spheres. Several examples in this chapter show how difficult it is to make a clear-cut distinction between the two spheres. The immigrant centre can in many ways be seen as semi-private (combining an external, administrative profile, as well as a profile of 'homeliness' where the women can cook, chat and sew). Some activities, however, are strictly public (i.e. administrative), while others are homely, as when the women cook together. Besides underlining the fuzzy border zone between private and public, the example also shows that the politics of and conflicts over space are not exclusively public phenomena. Negotiations over space are not restricted to streets, squares and alleys: the very same social processes seep into apartments, such as the one owned by the immigrant women's centre, and probably the other way around.

The Politics of Heterogeneous Spaces

Nørrebro is an excellent example of urban space as both (culturally) heterogeneous and, through this heterogeneity, inherently political. Public and urban spaces are, in the words of Doreen Massey (referring to R. Deutsche), 'the social space where, in the absence of a foundation, the meaning and unity of the social is negotiated – at once constituted and put at risk' (Massey, 2005, p. 153).

The arenas in which negotiations over space take place are multiple. In this chapter I have focused on one neighbourhood and the negotiations that take their starting point in religion, specifically based on the presence of a large community of Muslims (both Sunni and Shi'a) living in Nørrebro. Many more arenas and perspectives could be included: as already mentioned, Nørrebro is characterized by an abundance of subcultures, some based on ethnicity, others on class, and others again on ideology and religion. However, the role that religion plays in some of the encounters and negotiations is unquestionable. Religion is a field through which the unity of the social is negotiated – a process that also includes the element of risk and a situation where 'negotiation is forced upon us' (Massey, 2005, p. 154).

The element of risk is frequently associated with post-modern society. Risk arises when 'others' occupy or allow themselves to represent what other subjects understand as their 'territory of self', whether this territory implies national, religious or professional borders (Schmidt, 2008). Such territories of self do become less complex – and potentially inwardly and outwardly negotiable – within the heterogeneous space of the city. The sense of risk stems from precisely the experience that negotiation is not an option to run away from, a negotiation that may eventually result in the transformation and transfiguration of the imagery of the 'territory of self'.

What is at stake here is that while the city is perhaps inherently heterogeneous, conflictual and diverse, people seldom perceive or present themselves that way. And although several of my informants praised – and several of my fieldwork observations stressed – the diverse aspects of Nørrebro, seeing them as a prerequisite for the neighbourhood's open attitude, such understandings also had their limitations. People formulated some of these limitations in and through space, for example, when expressing the need to have a place they could call their own. Such places could be an office space, as expressed by the health-care workers, or when Maya and others demanded the right to play music or pray in the corner of a women's centre. In other instances limitations were advocated more aggressively, as the examples from the Open House events in Wakf indicated. Similarly, we can see the Shi'a procession as a means, through its use of space, to counter understandings of the identity-based limitations that some argued that Nørrebro includes.

In the end, the examples, statements and analyses in this chapter invite us to think in terms of another element of space than those of heterogeneity and diversity: that of home. Ultimately, the 'social' negotiated in urban spaces is the sense of being and belonging. It is the feeling of home and being at home. Including aspects of the private in the map of the city pushes the argument further. The city is about public spaces, but city spaces are interlinked and include people who move in and out of houses where they live with their spouses, children or parents, in so far as they do not live alone. When they go out, they bring what is private with them. And when they return home, they bring what is public back with them. Privacy is also a part of urban street life, including personal and group-based imaginations of what these streets include as home.

The (grounded) politics of space is, indeed, about negotiations, conflicts and statements of identity. But such processes also highlight the search for and state a goal – which can be the stating of home. Sometimes this statement points back in time, towards a nostalgic longing for belonging. In other instances, statements and negotiations voiced and embodied in and through space point to the ambition to stress certain aspects of the city's diversity as inherent and indispensable parts of the city. Several of the examples I have given in this chapter stress this perspective. The content of space is diverse, but through the lens of home aspects of space are associated (or are advocated to contain) the quality of inherent and unquestionable belonging.

References

Algren, L. (1999) *Nørrebro – gennem den multikulturelle by.* Copenhagen: Mellemfolkeligt Samvirke.
Amit, V. (2010) *Community as 'Good to Think With': The Productiveness of Strategic Ambiguities.* Lecture at SFI – the Danish National Centre for Social Research, August 24.
Bernstein, M. (1997). Celebration and Suppression: The Strategic Uses of Identity by the Lesbian and Gay Movement. *American Journal of Sociology* 103 (3), pp. 531-565
Bourdieu, P., and L. J. D. Wacquant (1992). *An Invitation to Reflexive Sociology.* Chicago: The University of Chicago Press.
Danske muslimer markerer Ashura (2009). Retrieved from http://www.dr.dk/Nyheder/Indland/2009/12/27/183400.htm
Deutsche, R. (1996). *Evictions: Art and Spatial Politics.* Cambridge, MA: MIT Press.
Federspiel S., Jensen, K. S., and Wenzel, J. (1997). *Nørrebro – træk af en bydels historie.* Copenhagen: Knuths Forlag.
Glick Schiller, N., A. Cağlar and T. C. Guldbrandsen (2006). Beyond the Ethnic Lens: Locality, Globality and Born-Again Incorporation. *American Ethnologist*, vol. 33, no. 4. pp. 612-633.
Glick Schiller, N., and A. Cağlar (2009). Towards a Comparative Theory of Locality in Migration Studies: Incorporation and City Scale. *Journal of Ethnic and Migration Studies*, vol. 35, no. 2. pp. 177-202.

Glick Schiller, N. (2008). *Beyond Methodological Ethnicity: Local and Transnational Pathways of Immigrant Incorporation*. Willy Brandt Series of Working Papers in International Migration and Ethnic Relations, 2/08. Malmö: Malmö University.

Grøndahl, M., K. Sinclair and T. R. Rasmussen (2003). *Hizb ut-Tahrir i Danmark: Farlig fundamentalisme eller uskyldigt ungdomsoprør?* Århus: Aarhus Universitetsforlag.

Hubbard, Ph., R. Kitchin and G. Valentine (2004). *Key Thinkers on Space and Place*. London: Sage.

Laclau, E. (1990). *New Reflections on the Revolution of Our Times*. London: Verso.

Lincoln, B. (1994). *Authority: Construction and Corrosion*. Chicago: The University of Chicago Press.

Massey, D. (2005). *For Space*. London: Sage.

"Erklæring: Sandheden bag urolighederne" (2008) Retrieved from http://politiken.dk/indland/fakta_indland/article473096.ece

Schmidt, G. (2007). Muslim i Danmark, Muslim i Verden: En analyse af muslimske ungdomsforeninger og muslimsk identitet i årene op til Muhammed-krisen. *Uppsala: Swedish Science Press.*

–, (2008). From Granting the Right (?!) Answers to Posing Odd Questions: Perspectives on Studying Muslim Minorities in a Politicized, Western Context. *Tidsskrift for Islamforskning i Danmark,* no. 2.

Statistics Copenhagen (2008). Befolkning efter bydel, herkomst, oprindelsesland og alder 1. januar 2008. Retrieved from http://www.sk.kk.dk/data2008/bydel08/befolkning/bef_indv_efterkom_oprindelsesland_alder_08.htm.

Stepick, A., T. Rey, S. J. Mahler (2009). *Churches and Charity in the Immigrant City: Religion, Immigration, and Civic Engagement in Miami*. New Brunswick: Rutgers University Press.

Vertovec, S. (2007). 'Super-Diversity and its Implications'. In *Ethnic and Racial Studies*, Vol. 30, no. 6. pp. 102-104.

Whose Courtroom? Observations from Terrorism Trials

Ann-Sophie Hemmingsen

Introduction

During five trials under Danish terrorism legislation[1] there was ample opportunity to observe the many individuals who followed the trials from the galleries. These observations provided interesting insights into how courtrooms are not merely physical settings for legal proceedings in which truth and evidence are negotiated and sentences are passed but also places in which participants and spectators negotiate relations and positions, attempt to continue their routines and uphold their values, opinions and points of views. In short places in which life is lived.

Courtrooms are supposedly neutral places where it is obvious who is *in place* and who is *out of place*. Representatives of the law – judges, jury, lawyers and others directly involved in the proceedings are *in place* and so are the spectators who abide by the rules by getting up for the judges and the jury and remaining

---

1 These five trials are: 1: The case against a young man, EIH, accused of having participated in planning a terrorist act, for which three individuals have been convicted in Bosnia and one in Denmark. This case is commonly named the Glostrup-case in Denmark whereas it is also known as the Sarajevo plot in international context. The Danish case began in 2006 where four men were accused of having planned a terrorist attack and temporarily ended in 2007 when the jury found all four men guilty but the judges overruled the jury in three of the cases and found only one man guilty. As a consequence the case against the three remaining men was to continue with new judges and jurors but the prosecutor decided to drop the charges against two of the three and only uphold it against one, EIH. This case began on 7 January 2008 and ended on 10 March 2008 with the complete acquittal of EIH. 2: The case against two men, HK and AT, accused of having planned a terrorist attack and among other things having manufactured the explosive TATP. This case is commonly known as the Glasvej-case. The case ended on 21 October 2008 when the two men were found guilty and sentenced to twelve and seven years. 3: The appeal of the Glasvej-case which ended 26 July 2009 when the two men were once again found guilty and sentenced to twelve and eight years. 4: This case was an offshoot from the Glasvej-case. A young man, SÜ, was accused of planning a terrorist attack by ordering an individual to arrange the kidnapping of Danish soldiers. According to the prosecutors his plan was to use the kidnapping of these soldiers to coerce Danish authorities to abstain from prosecuting the two men charged in the Glasvej-case. The court case ended on 18 November 2008 with acquittal. 5: the appeal of this case which ended with acquittal 28 August 2009. Following these trials is part of an extensive fieldwork carried out in 2008 and 2009 in collaboration with Dr. Manni Crone, Danish Institute for International Studies.

silent when the court is in session. Spectators and defendants who do not abide by those rules are *out of place*. But through the five trials this dichotomy became less clear. The individuals present were not simply representatives of the law, defendants, or spectators and the courtrooms were more than simply physical settings for legal proceedings with clear rules. They were also spaces in which life – for limited periods of time – was lived by all those present. Life in these supposedly neutral places was lived in ways shaped not only by the places but also by the individuals present in them.

Danish courtrooms are decorated in ways that are clearly intended to strip them of any apparent references to religion or other non-legal symbolism but during these trials they were filled with religious symbolism. Many of the individuals present carried religion on their sleeve. The atmosphere in Danish courtrooms is quite discreet and toned down. Objections are delivered in a quit and restrained manner and voices are rarely raised – unlike in American movies. Many of the individuals present broke this style and were noisy and made interruptions. Such contrasts occasionally led to virtual symbolic battles over whose space the courtroom was.

The present article revolves around observations of such individuals[2] and explores how Doreen Massey's and Tim Cresswell's conceptualizations of *lived space* can contribute to the analyses of what might appear to be inappropriate or even incomprehensible behaviour if viewed solely as bystanders' reactions and

---

2   These individuals fall under the category often described as *Salafi Jihadis*. Salafism is characterised by a strict interpretation of Islam in which great emphasis is put on practise and on imitation of the Prophet Muhammad, his companions and the three first Caliphs. Guidelines for this are primarily found in *Hadith* and *Sunnah*. Hadith is written collections on the life, actions, words and rulings of the prophet whereas Sunnah is the ways and behaviours of the Prophet and his companions – the *Sahaba*. Sunnah is primarily found in Hadith. Sunnah includes very specific acts, phrases and traditions of the Prophet and the Sahaba and to Salafis these are crucial – they are what sometimes make it possible to distinguish Salafis from other Muslims. Among the most commonly known physical indications are clothes – such as trousers that do not cover the ankles – and full beards. The traditions also include details in the way prayer is performed e.g. maintaining a straight back at all times and adding words to the prayer, and rules for sharing and receiving gifts, for greeting and for entering a room. Salafis put great emphasis on distancing themselves from anything which is not sanctioned by the Quran, Hadith and Sunnah, which means that they do not accept democracy and laws other than the Islamic law *Sharia* as these are viewed as created by man end therefore fundamentally flawed since man is incapable of separating himself from his own desires and interests whereas God has handed down the perfect systems and guidelines. Modern Salafis disagree internally on how to handle their surroundings and particularly the fact that they all live in societies which do not live up to their expectations. Some deal with this by separating themselves entirely from surrounding society, others attempt to engage in political processes to change the systems from within and a very small minority believes that status quo must be fought by violent means which they justify by reference to the concept Jihad. These are the ones commonly referred to as *Jihadis* – hence the conceptualization of them as Salafi Jihadis. For much more on this see Wiktorowicz, 2006.

responses to legal proceedings in the neutral and highly institutionalized settings of courtrooms.

Lived Spaces

I draw on Massey's and Cresswell's understanding of place as something dynamic which is continuously negotiated and constructed by individuals inhabiting it. This implies that no place is something in essence – places only become something once human beings assign meaning to them. This further implies that all places can change. They can remain the same if all individuals inhabiting them agree on what they are and practise – or use – them in a consistent manner but once an individual questions the meaning of a place or practises it in a different manner the place changes.

> "Place, in other words does – as many argue – change us, not through some visceral belonging (some barely changing rootedness, as so many would have it) but through the *practising* of place, the negotiation of intersecting trajectories; place as an arena where negotiation is forced upon us" (Italics in original text. (Massey, 2005, p. 154))

Places, however, are not only affected by how they are practised – they also affect what can be practised in them. Places and the practising of them are part of an ever evolving negotiation where the previously existing practises affect and are affected by new ones. This is referred to as *lived space* – something emerging when dissimilar individuals find themselves in the same place forcing them to relate to each other.

> "In these terms bodies and places are never established. They only operate through constant and reiterative practice. They are produced as much as they are producing. Indeed they are performed. Every single day, everywhere, places need to be reproduced. They exist, they surround and inform our practice and we cannot get away from that. […] they produce a sense of limits. They are as Bourdieu would put it 'structured structures predisposed to act as structuring structures'" (Bourdieu, 1990, p. 83; Cresswell, 2002, p. 23).

Both Massey and Cresswell also hold that place and lived space is inherently linked to politics and power. I do not intend to enter the discussion on this aspect of the theorising on human geography but simply contend that since the places which this article revolves around – courtrooms during trials under terrorism legislation – are surely infused with politics, power and contestation of power this understanding appears helpful. In the courtrooms representatives of the authorities are obviously in power. The court has the power to judge and pass sentences and to decide who is allowed to be present in the courtroom as spectators. The police have the power to decide who enters and exits, they have the power to search and register spectators and demand that they leave their personal belongings in the police's custody – and they have weapons.

The context of the actual trials is political in essence – it is a political act to define something as terrorism and it is a political decision to trial defendants under terrorism legislation which is made by the Danish Minister of Justice. Within these frames there is a clear division between who is the majority, in power and therefore deciding which behaviour is correct and then who is the minority who is expected to conform.

In the following I will first attempt to describe the physical settings for the observations – the courtrooms – to set the scene. I will then provide six examples of observations from terrorism trials and one example from another type of trial to illustrate how much more than legal proceedings take place in and around the courtrooms. Finally, I will explore how the conceptualizations of lived space can contribute to understanding what may appear to be inappropriate or even incomprehensible behaviour.

The Courtrooms

Even before one enters the buildings where the courtrooms are situated the scene is set during terrorism trials. The streets surrounding the buildings are regulated by heavily armed police, hardly noticeable snipers are stationed on rooftops and when the defendants are transported to and from the courts the streets are blocked. Police patrol the area, they stop individuals attempting to pass by and conduct searches on a regular basis. Entry into the actual area of the court buildings is further restricted by heavily armed police requiring justification for entering the premises. Once having been allowed to enter the premises even more heavily armed police appear. The entrances to the court buildings and to the actual courtrooms are guarded and spectators are required to pass through metal detectors and thorough searches. Spectators are then instructed to hand over personal belongings and provide identification, including social security numbers which is registered. What spectators are allowed to bring into the courtroom – and out during breaks – varies. Sometimes they are allowed to bring everything except mobile phones and objects made of metal (e.g. coins, keys and nail files) into the courtroom and allowed to bring the mobile phone outside during breaks. At other times even getting to bring in a pen and paper is a difficult task – on these days the police also forbid beverages in the courtroom and mobile phones during breaks and even limit the number of cigarettes spectators are allowed to bring with them during breaks. There does not appear to be any system guiding these variations.

Having passed through these obstacles the spectator finally enters the courtroom. The trials I have followed have been held in four different courtrooms but the lay-out of all of them have followed certain patterns setting the scene for the proceedings and establishing authority.

The judges wear black cloaks which are long enough to cover their knees and hide most of their clothes. Prosecutor and defence wear the same cloaks but the prosecutors' cloaks have purple trimmings along all edges and the defences' have red trimmings.

When entering the courtroom, one finds the seating for the three judges slightly elevated from the rest of the room. To one side one finds the seating for the jury arranged in two rows and next to them is the prosecutor and his/her assistances. To the other side of the judges – and opposite to the prosecutor and the jury – one finds the defendants and their defence. In front of the judges – and in the centre of the room between jury, prosecutor, defendants and defence – is the seat for witnesses and behind this is the gallery where journalists, friends, family and others can observe in silence. Usually there is a table at the front of this gallery which is reserved for journalists. Behind the various participants in the trial are bookshelves with folders containing the documents for the proceedings. The courtrooms are usually decorated in neutral colours and feature abstract works of art upon which the eye can find ease.

The defendants are brought into the courtroom by guards. Sometimes the guards are heavily armed and the defendants are wearing bulletproof vests, chains and handcuffs and at other times the guards are in ordinary uniforms and the defendants are almost free to move about. I have observed the same individual being brought into one courtroom as a witness with high level security measures one day and into another courtroom as a defendant shortly after with no security measures. I have also observed the security measures drastically decline over the course of a single trial.

What does not change, however, is the fact that once the guards have brought in the defendants and the doors have been closed behind them six to ten police officers stay in the courtroom during the proceedings. The sense of an imminent threat rarely leaves the room.

Life in the Courtrooms

These courtrooms are surely places in which different trajectories intersect and stages on which negotiations are forced upon all individuals present. The places set a certain agenda and to some extent shape what can go on in them – which negotiations can take place and how. When individuals challenge these places' authority the challenges are not unaffected by the very places. But even these highly institutionalised places are not static or unaffected either – they do not simply remain the same through these negotiations. To illustrate this and how the space is lived and negotiated I shall now introduce six examples of observations from terrorism trials and one example of observations from another type of trial.

Dress Codes

The objects of my observations wear religion on their sleeve. They do this figuratively by their behaviour but they also do so quite literally. It would appear that there are certain *dress codes* when it comes to physical appearances, i.e. clothes, beards, hair etc. One can wear oversized street wear, more ordinary jeans or cargo pants – both without covering the ankles – or the Saudi *thawb*[3] or other traditional Arabian or South-East-Asian attires. The uncovered ankles and the entire dress codes are ways of signalling that one belongs to a certain creed often referred to as Salafi[4]. All of these may then be combined with crochet hats, impressive beards and – for the ones who are the most cutting edge: long hair[5].

For the ladies the repertoire is somewhat more limited. As a minimum everything except face and hands must be covered by clothing or preferably by what is referred to as *Somali-style* garments[6] or *niqabs*[7]. As one explained to me; these are *Sunnah*-clothes[8].

These dress codes are used very consciously: one individual had shaved off his beard and controlled his hair in a bun during his own trial but as a spectator during later trials he followed the abovementioned dress codes. Another individual had a full beard when summoned to give testimony in a trial at a point in time when he himself was in pre-trial detention but was clean-shaven during his own trial a few months later. A third individual wore clothes which could best be described as according to the dress code known as *business casual* when summoned to give testimony during a trial but abided to the abovementioned dress code for the later verdict of that trial. It appears obvious that the participants are quite aware of the risks associated with standing out in this way.

This specific dress code is surely an integral part of how my objects of observation practice religion but dress codes are in no way unusual. Physical appearances are commonly used to signal group affiliation –examples could be skinheads, punks etc. Nevertheless, the fact that my objects of observation are appa-

---

3 A long white shirt.
4 For a thorough introduction to Salafism and the various factions see Wiktorowicz, 2006.
5 For more on the meaning and importance of appearances see Rougier, 2008.
6 A garment made from a single piece of cloth which covers everything except hands and face.
7 An attire which includes a piece of cloth covering the face below the eyes.
8 I.e. clothes comparable to those worn by the Prophet and his companions.

rently aware that some occasions are more favourable than others for making such signals tells us something about the lived space in the courtroom. There is a negotiation going on between the formalised clothing of judges and lawyers and the clothing of my objects of observation. This negotiation is not only related to the trials going on in the courtrooms. It is related to a disagreement about what is appropriate in courtrooms but also about what is appropriate in life in general.

As mentioned, spectators are subjected to searches when entering the courtrooms. Searches of females are carried out by female police officers and searches of males are carried out by male police officers, but they take place in public. This often led to ladies asking the officers to not reveal their legs or the shape of their body when searching them. On several occasions such requests were attempted met and the officers placed large bookcases to create shielded areas where females could be searched.

Overruling Authority?

When the judges and the jury enter the courtroom everybody is expected to get up as a sign of respect of their authority and the very authority of the trial and at the beginning of each day in court the presiding judge often states that outbursts and other interruptions will not be accepted. Individuals who fail to comply with these rules can be expelled from the courtroom. Nevertheless, many quite creative breaches of these rules were performed but not once did I witness an individual being expelled.

The most obvious type of breach was individuals who refused to get up when the judges and the jury entered the room. A refinement of this silent protest developed over the course of the trials I attended. During the first trials some individuals simply remained seated without attempting to hide it but this led to warnings from the judges or the police present in the courtrooms so alternative strategies emerged. One such strategy was dropping something on the floor and then picking it up or tying shoelaces which were not undone when the judges and the jury entered. Another strategy was for individuals who had attended many sessions in court and refused to get up and stand in front of others who remained seated hidden by the ones standing. This strategy possibly also served the purpose of the newcomers proving their willingness to participate and take risks and the experienced ones bolstering their status. Yet another type of breaches was somewhat more inventive. Chanting, singing or reciting from the Quran, burping and farting, or laughing when the prosecutor was presenting evidence – such as surveillance videos of the defendants or their downloaded videos featuring executions – are among the examples. Finally, getting up when defendants or witnesses enter the room is an act in obvious contrast to the refusal to get up for the judges and the jury.

Such behaviour is not always performed with the same enthusiasm. It is quite obvious that there are a few individuals who are skilled at staging it and leading the others. It is also obvious that the enthusiasm increases the more peers are present. This became very clear during the last trial I attended.

On the first day, three young men entered the courtroom all dressed up and ready to perform. But before the court was set the defendant's lawyer approached one of them and asked him to leave the court because they wanted him to give testimony later. This young man was one of the most active in arranging protests and after his exit the two remaining men did not make much of an effort. At the end of the day I overheard them agreeing to reappear the next day but they did not.

It also became clear during another trial when an individual – who had just been released after serving a three and a half year sentence for inciting to terrorism – turned up and performed the routine with not getting up while pretending to tie his shoelaces. He only lasted one day – perhaps because there were no peers who joined or appreciated the protest. In fact, the only response was the prosecutor scolding him in the courtroom. Incidentally, this individual may in fact have been the one setting the standard for performance in courtrooms when he appeared during his own trial wearing an orange T-shirt with the text "Guantanamo".

These performances appear to be protests against – and lack of recognition of – the authority of the court. On closer inspection, however, they also appear to be directed at the peers and to be a part of living life the way that my objects of observation see fit.

The first times I witnessed spectators burping and farting during the trials I interpreted it as blatant provocations and obvious disrespect of the court. But through conversations with some of the individuals who had taken part in the behaviour I learned that they did not necessarily see it this way. As one of them explained: "your body has privileges over you."[9] He further explained that this meant that since our bodies belong to Allah we are obliged to take care of them, respect them, fulfil their needs and allow them to function even if doing so collides with our own wishes or desires. This implies that we are not allowed to smoke or do anything else that we know is harmful to our bodies but it also implies that when the body has natural needs and functions we must accommodate them rather than denying them to e.g. protect our pride or behave according to customs or expectations. In this line of thinking burping or farting in court is not necessarily directed at the court it may just as well be a continuation of living life the way that some see fit.

---

9   Interview 1 July 2009.

The Perfect Host

The final day of these trials is always somewhat hectic. Many family members and friends are present but often a large number of journalists also swarm the premises with their cameras attempting to get the best pictures and interviews. On the final day of one trial the attendance was far too great and many were held back from entering the court building, including family members of one of the defendants. The information that this was the case reached the courtroom on the third floor and in the gallery great efforts were put into arranging more seats and counting how many were then available. Dispatches were then sent down to the police at the entrance to tell them that there was now room for a few more. The police then let in a final group including the family members. When this group entered the courtroom one individual in the gallery took it upon him to arrange the seating and move people around so that the seating was appropriate according to his standards. The police present in the courtroom did not approve of this service. This individual had previously showed such skills when commanding his friends to let the family members of defendants, women and elderly enter the courtroom before they did, arranging chairs for family members when we sometimes had to wait to be let into the courtroom and ensuring that women could be seated together. This rarely went unnoticed by police and prosecutor. He was often pulled aside and instructed that he was not in charge of this place and told to behave if he wanted to stay. Nevertheless, his arrangements were usually allowed to remain in force which indicates that he to some extent was the successful party of the negotiations over who was allowed to define appropriate behaviour in court.

Protest Prayers?

At the end of a long day of a trial I stumbled into a surprising event. I was leaving the court building which was heavily populated with more than 50 policemen in full gear and machineguns. The area was cordoned off by concrete barriers etc. for security reasons and in front of these barriers were heavily armed policemen. As I passed through to one of the exits I noticed two of the young men who was following the trial standing in front of the barrier and one was taking of his jacket. He greeted me wishing me a safe trip home and explained that he had missed his prayers and was going to perform one now. I probably looked quite surprised and asked him, sceptically, here? He replied, laughing, that he was indeed going to perform his prayer here and added that he was the safest he had ever been – they were all taking such good care of him. At this point in time, a baffled policeman – with his machinegun in his hand – had taken notice and began approaching us with a very bewildered look on his face and the other policemen present were looking to each other clearly as unsure of how to handle the situation. We said our goodbyes agreeing that we would meet again the next day – the policemen still looking bewildered. As I left the scene I heard the young man calling "Allahu akhbar" and as I turned around I saw him kneeling on the ground – the policemen were not looking any less bewildered.

The following days the performing of prayers in and around the court house increased. Rather than being postponed till the end of the day the prayers were performed during the breaks and inside the court house in the corridors by an increasing number of young men but none as blatantly spectacular as the first.

It stands to reason that the first young man chose the stage for his prayer in order to be able to show his lack of fear and respect of the police but had this been the only motive for performing prayers in and around the court buildings one would have expected the following performances of prayers to be increasingly confrontational in style – or at least as confrontational as the first. Since this was not the case it is reasonable to assume that the prayer served more than this one purpose. By performing the initial prayer the young man made a breakaway from the predominant atmosphere in and around the courtrooms – he showed that prayers in this place were an option and by doing so made them a part of the negotiations over what is appropriate behaviour.

Enjoying the Sun

The days in court are somewhat structured around breaks. The court is set at 9 am and around 10.30 there is a 15 minute break. At noon there is a one hour lunch break and at around 2 pm there is another 15 minute break. Usually the day ends at 3 pm. This structure means that spectators need not be present all day but can join and leave during the breaks.

On one of the last days of a trial we exited the courtroom during the first break and encountered an unusual sight: in the hall in front of the courtroom a young lady was sleeping on a bench. She was wearing a bright red Somali-style garment. The police guarding the entrance were obviously uncomfortable and with apologetic smiles glanced at her and all of us exiting the courtroom. This was not the behaviour one would expect in a court building in Copenhagen, particularly during a trial under such heavy security measures, and it was not the behaviour one would expect from a lady wearing that type of clothes. She showed guts – she was not impressed by the setting, she was not impressed by the armed police and she was not limited by what is expected of a lady covered from top to toe. She was tired and played by her own rules.

Later that day came the lunch break. The lady in red, my colleague and I went to the cafeteria in the court building and bought food. In the cafeteria there was a buffet and the young lady effectively involved the staff in picking out appropriate foods – which dishes were *halal*, and were they really halal or just factory-halal where non-Muslims had worked under halal-rules? We finally had a satisfactory selection and went out to the lawn and joined two men and she altruistically shared her food with all of us. When we were done eating the lady in red made herself comfortable by lying down on the lawn to enjoy the sun.

After a while another young lady joined us. She was wearing an ordinary hijab and trousers but apparently took offence by the lady in red's behaviour. She politely asked her to behave in a respectable manner when she was dressed the way she was. She went on to explain that the way a woman behaves when wearing a bikini is her own business but when a woman is dressed in "this way" she should behave in certain, appropriate ways. The lady in red politely asked her what she meant by respectable and appropriate. The other lady tried to explain how she should not lie down but sit up straight with her legs to one side. The lady in red then asked where she had found those rules – if it was in Islam or in culture. The other lady – now obviously uncomfortable – held her ground and replied that there are certain ways a lady should behave and that this is a way of showing respect. The lady in red replied by stating that she did not mean any disrespect but she only abided by the rules of Islam, she did not accept culture or tradition. If the other lady could provide her with appropriate sources for her commands she would greatly appreciate it. The discussion ended peacefully and later that day the lady in red explained to me what it had been about.

Most Muslims, in her view, follow traditions which have nothing to do with Islam and this is most harmful. Only rules and commands which can be found in the Quran, Hadith or Sunnah are to be followed and if one individual commands another to behave in a certain way it is the duty of the former to provide such sources – the other individual is not obliged to abide until they have been provided, neither is he or she obliged to investigate whether the sources exist.

She later expanded on the dimensions of this subject by explaining how many women from Somalia have been subjected to genital mutilation because their parents believe this to be commanded in Islam – which she assured me was incorrect. This interpretation resonates with the views on bodily needs and functions introduced above under the headline *Overruling authority?* Both represent a breakaway from conforming to social norms.

This observation illustrates how negotiations are not necessarily limited to negotiations between representatives of the court and representatives of the spectators who challenge the court. They can also be between spectators who disagreed on how one is to behave and live. This means that the boundaries of groups are fluid and change. The two ladies who discussed appropriate behaviour were sometimes part of the same group – e.g. Muslim women following a terrorism trial or acquaintances of defendants – but during this discussion they were suddenly parts of two conflicting groups.

The Other Side

Representatives of the authorities, i.e. police and the prosecutor, often engage directly in the battle over whose space the courtroom is. On many occasions I have witnessed police officers and prosecutors engaging by informing *the usual suspects* that: "we call the shots in this courtroom" and "if you do not get up for the judges and the jury you will be thrown out". It can also be done by pulling them to the side when we are waiting in line and holding them back until everybody else has entered the courtroom, to tell them to behave. They also engage in the battles in non-verbal ways by placing big police officers next to them in the gallery, by searching them and their cars in the area around the court buildings, by holding them back from entering the courtroom, by searching them even more thoroughly than the rest of us, taking more of their belongings away, refusing to hand them back etc.

The strife over whether religious symbolism has a place in courtrooms is not limited to the symbolic battles in courtrooms during trials under terrorism legislation. Like many other countries Denmark has seen a – sometimes quite heated – debate on headscarves in the public sphere. In 2007 it became an issue that, in theory, judges in Danish courtrooms could wear a hijab. Politicians then suggested a law which could prevent this from happening. This provoked responses from the legal profession and four defence lawyers – three male and one female – appeared in a city court in January 2009 wearing hijabs (Astrup, 2009).

But the protests were futile and on 1 July 2009 a law was passed establishing that judges may not present themselves in courts in ways that are "fit to be perceived as an expression of their eventual religious or political affiliations or attitudes towards religious or political matters"[10].

A Different Type of Trials

During these trials there are of course also individuals present on the gallery who are not Salafi Jihadis. There are representatives of intelligence services who wish

---

10   Law no. 495, 2009:§56

to gain insight into the cases, there are journalists, the occasional lawyers and students, spectators who are interested in the cases and there are family members and friends of the defendants. These individuals have different points of views and in the words of Massey different trajectories. They bring something else to the dynamics of the courtrooms – they too take part in living the space.

To better understand the dynamics of these trials I occasionally sat in on other trials under entirely different legislation than terrorism. One such trial which provided good contrasts was about two police officers who had shot and killed a man who attempted to escape them in a car with a fugitive suspected of murder as passenger. This trial took place in the same courtroom as one of the trials under terrorism legislation would later take place – the courtroom described above as obviously redecorated for the occasion.

During this trial the galley was primarily occupied by family and friends of the victim who to some extent also represented a culture which is in conflict with majority society. But this group of people nonetheless accepted and respected the rule of law and the court's authority.

The first thing that caught the eye was the absence of security measures in and around the courtroom. Since this was a case where one individual had been killed and another was suspected of murder the relaxed atmosphere was something of a surprise.

The second thing that caught the eye was the extent to which everybody in the courtroom abided by the rules of the court. Not one individual refused to get up for the judges or made rude comments about the proceedings or the situation in spite of the fact that this was a case where representatives of the authorities had killed their family member or friend. Even when the judges ruled that the two police officers had done nothing wrong it was accepted without much more than tears.

Life in the same place was lived in quite different ways not because of the place but because of the individuals present in it.

Courtrooms as Lived Spaces

Many of the observed negotiations at first sight appear to be directed at representatives of the court and thereby – to some extent – to be related to the trials. But on closer inspection it appears reasonable to interpret some of these negotiations as being directed as much towards peers as towards representatives of the court.

Some of the observed negotiations quite obviously had little or nothing to do with the trials at all. Examples of the latter would be the negotiations between to women over how to behave in a public place and the search for appropriate dishes in the cafeteria.

When my objects of observation refused to abide by the rules of the court by not getting up when the judges and jury entered, by commenting and being noisy during proceedings, etc. they were surely attempting to show that they challenged the authority of the court but the audience of these challenges was not solely representatives of the court. The fact that these challenges were performed more often and with more enthusiasm when peers were present and responding indicates that they were also intended for this audience.

The same appears to be the case with the observations of *the perfect host*. When he had been corrected and instructed to abide by the rules of the court by representatives of the court he would return to his peers and report which indicates that their reaction was important too as was their participation.

When the same individual performed prayer in the midst of heavily armed police in front of the court building he was surely intending to show his lack of fear of them but when the performing of prayer in and around the court house increased over the following days it did not appear to be intended solely for representatives of the court or other authorities.

The observations illustrated how some forms of behaviour served several purposes. One such purpose was to challenge the authority of the courts – directly by not abiding to the rules thereby showing disrespect but also less obviously by behaving in ways perceived to be inappropriate and thereby challenging the majority's right to define what appropriate behaviour in a courtroom is.

Another purpose was that some individuals claimed the space – in the courtrooms – as space in which they could continue life as they saw fit.

Sometimes the results of the negotiations were in favour of my objects of observation. This could be observed in a quite direct way when the police created shielded areas where women could be searched and in a less direct way when the instructions given by *the perfect host* were allowed to remain in force.

The observations also illustrated how negotiations were not limited to negotiations between representatives of the court and representatives of the spectators who challenged the court. There were also negotiations between spectators who disagreed on how one was to behave, e.g. as a woman. As a consequence the boundaries of groups shifted and individuals who at one point in time appeared to be part of a group, e.g. spectators who do not comply with the rules, at other points in time appeared to be parts of separate groups and even conflicting groups.

As the lawyers who appeared in a Danish courtroom wearing hijabs illustrate, the interest in negotiations about the appropriateness of religious symbols in courtrooms is not limited to my objects of observation – neither is the willingness to participate in negotiations about more than the matters of guilt and law in courtrooms.

What might appear to be inappropriate or even incomprehensible behaviour if viewed solely as bystanders' reactions and responses to legal proceedings in the neutral and highly institutionalized settings of courtrooms becomes less inappropriate and incomprehensible when interpreted as more than that.

As the described examples of observations from five trial under Danish terrorism legislation illustrate, courtrooms are not only neutral, physical settings for legal proceedings but also places in which life is being lived for limited periods of time – like all other places.

References

Astrup, E.(2009). Advokater tog tørklæde på i retten ("Lawyers wore veils in court"), *Politiken*. Retrieved from: http://politiken.dk/indland/article636473.ece January 26.

Cresswell, T. (2004). *Place. A Short Introduction*. Malden: Blackwell

–, (1996). *In Place/Out of Place: Geography, Ideology and Transgression*. Minneapolis: University of Minnesota Press

Cresswell, T. & Verstraete, G. (2002). (Eds.). *Mobilizing Place, Placing Mobility: The Politics of Representation in a Globalized World*. Amsterdam: Rodopi

Massey, D. (2005). *For Space*. London: Sage Law no. 495 (2009, June 12) "Retsplejeloven" ("Administration of Justice Act"), Retrieved from: https://www.retsinformation.dk/Forms/R0710.aspx?id=125401

Rougier, B (2008). *Qu'est-ce que le salafisme?* Paris: Presse Universitaires de France

Wiktorowicz, Q. (2006). Anatomy of the Salafi Movement. *Studies in Conflict and Terrorism*, 29, pp. 207-239

Trans-National Islamic TV: A Space for Religious and Gendered Living

Ehab Galal

Introduction

Since the beginning of the nineties, the number of Arab Islamic satellite television channels has grown explosively and so has the variety of programmes (Galal, 2009). European politicians and observers have stressed their fear that satellite television might affect processes of integration negatively, due to the channels' alleged promotion of radicalisation and islamisation. Thus, they seem to take for granted a deterministic relation between what people see on television, what they believe in, and how they practice their life. The content of the diverse programmes have, though, only to a lesser degree been examined. Likewise, the relationship between the audience and the programmes has not been explored and only a few fragmented and limited reception analyses have been carried out (Amin, 2008). Consequently, very little is known about the audience's use of Islamic satellite television. However, as media researchers have suggested a "re-enchantment" of public spheres, partly due to the return of religion in the media, the media has increasingly been examined as a *place* or *space* for religious identity representations, constructions and practices (cf. Martín-Barbero, 1997; Murdock, 1997; Hoover, 2006). From this perspective follows that the media broadcast is not only a representation of reality, rather media is one of several places where religion and religious identities are practiced and lived. Thus, a key issue is how the audience makes use of the media as a place for identity formation and social practices.

Part of the Islamic satellite channels' potential audience is Arabic-speaking immigrants and their descendants in Europe. I write 'potential', because we do have very limited knowledge about the Islamic channels' audience within or outside the Arab world. Judged from the phone-in programmes, though a European audience, mostly are immigrants with Arab origins. To be an immigrant often means to be bi- or multilingual and to identify with more than one nation or territorial locality (Levitt & Glick-Schiller, 2004). Furthermore, the immigrants can be considered minorities in the receiving country, as far as groups of immigrants very seldom have the power of definition in relation to norms, values, and what is considered normal within the national framework (Krag, 2007). They are not only subjects to the national law, regulations and institutions; they are also often constructed by the majority as subjects with specific moral obligations. They are expected not only to identify with national values and norms; they are – to some degree – expected, as well, to distance themselves from values and norms, which the majority considers related to their religious, cultural or ethnic origins as far as they are considered a threat against basic values of the host society (Andreassen, 2005).

Such moral obligations are for instance demands towards Muslim women by European societies. These are often within a politicised discourse rather rigid and related to her clothing, her position in the family and in society, and specifically to her supposed unequal relationship with her husband. Such demands are made in public through different kinds of educational initiatives and as political rhetoric. In a Danish context it seems to be a moral obligation to narrate gender and gender equality in a specific way, especially when it comes to the immigrant women. A result of this public discourse is discursive – if not legal – constraints on the Arab Muslim woman to live and practice other gender identities than the one morally defined by the European countries' national publics. The many debates on the use of hijab and burka illustrate this tendency. Furthermore, there seems to be limited room for practices where gender identities converge with a Muslim and immigrant identity and not least for narrations and negotiations of converging identities. Available places might be mosques, Muslim organisations, women clubs, private homes etc. Nevertheless, these are mainly locally embedded despite of possible transnational contacts and relations. In contrast, satellite television transgresses national borders and is what one would call globally embedded and transnational per se. Hence, the issue is in this connection what characterises the Islamic satellite television as a specific kind of transnational place or space? The questions are, how does the Islamic satellite television take up the challenge of offering a space, where Arab Muslim women can *live* their different identities simultaneously as Arab, Muslim, immigrant, and woman without the majority's interference? What characterises the space offered? Does it form an alternative to other Muslim spaces? How does it comply with the immigrants' experience of simultaneity, being Danish, Arab, minority, Muslim, and woman at the same time? And how does it answer the moral requirements defined by Europe to change your way of life, if you are a Muslim woman?

In order to answer these questions, the chapter proceeds as follows. To be able to discuss Islamic satellite television characteristics and potentially as lived spaces, I will give an account of the varied religious and gendered programming that Islamic TV is offering its transnational audience. I will argue that these programmes offer the Arab Muslim woman spaces for negotiating traditional views of the Muslim woman's space as being only the private home and sphere. At the same time the private space of home seems increasingly to be a subject of the satellite-television. Thus the private and public spaces seem to conflate and converge in the Islamic programming. As such, religious identity and practices, gender representation and meaning of place are intersecting on satellite television. This perspective raises a variety of questions to the meaning of place and space. In order to clarify my use of these concepts, I will to begin with shortly dwell on conventional constructions of the Muslim woman's role and its hegemonic status, as hitherto reproduced by Arab television. In so doing, I will – inspired by the discussion of Tim Cresswell (2002) – argue for an approach to television as not only a space for representations and images, but as a place for social practices: *a lived space*. Secondly, I will give an introduction to the development of Arab satellite-television and religious woman programmes trying to pin down the kinds of lived spaces being offered. Thirdly, I will analyse three different programme types on Iqraa to exemplify how new programming on Islamic satellite-television might become lived spaces. Finally, I am going to discuss and conclude how the lived spaces offered by Islamic transnational television have the potential to be a place where Arabic speaking women in European countries share lived experiences as Muslims and women.

Place and Identity Brought into Being

Looking at previous studies of women's representation in Arab media, the Muslim Arab woman seems to be presented through rather stereotypical picturing. Thus, media researcher Muhammed el-Omar (2006) has examined Syrian drama-serials and Nahed Ramzy (2004) has analysed the picturing of women in Egyptian cinema. Both studies find similar constructions of the Arab woman. She is first of all pictured as a wife, a mother, and a sister. Her role as a wife is characterised by dependence on her husband while she loves him and takes care of his comfort. Similar to the role as wife, the mother and sister have roles that are secondary roles to the man who decides their fate. However, if the woman is rich, she is pictured as dominant and obdurate. The mother as well as the daughter is pictured as loving, caring, and obedient. At the same time, the daughter's role is to find the suitable husband-to-be (El-Omar, 2006). Nahed Ramzy argues, in her study on the Egyptian cinema, that women are presented as passive while men are active; women are emotional, while men are rational. Women are presented as biological reproducers of the Nation, as well as protectors and transmitters of national cultural and religious traditions (Ramzy, 2004). In general, the gender of the woman is privileged by the producers by presenting it as a primary identity, which determines other identity characteristics of the individual Arab woman (El-Omar, 2006). In regard to women's life in the Arab world of today, Arab media, according to these studies, neither reflects the reality where women have gained professional and influential positions in Arab society, nor do they represent the cultural and social differences among Arab women within the particular Arab country in question or between different Arab countries (Ramzy, 2004, p. 94). If a professional woman is portrayed, she works just to fill her free time, or to meet economic needs. Women's work outside the home is never presented as valuable or meaningful in itself (El-Omar, 2006).

The question is then, if and how Islamic satellite television better complies with the reality of the Arab women of today. Some considerations have to be mentioned before clarifying the theoretical approach. These are related to the picturing of the Arab woman and its potential change due to satellite transmission. Not only is the object in question – the Islamic satellite channels – defining themselves as Islamic with Islamic values and as defenders of the Muslim family and community. But the Arab Muslim states also seek to control the outcome of transnational broadcasting. Even today, with generally more liberal media politics in the Arab countries, not only the national television[1], but also transnational television is restricted through common Arab media politics. Thus, the Arab ministers of information agreed in 2008 upon a new charter with the title: "Suggested Guidelines and Principles for Organizing Satellite TV in the Arab World" (Al-Tahhawi, 2008). It states a list of requirements to the satellite-channels:

"– not to offend the leaders or national and religious symbols in the Arab world; – not to damage social harmony, national unity, public order or traditional values; – to conform with the religious and ethical values of Arab society and take account of its family structure; – to refrain from broadcasting anything which calls into question God, the monotheistic-religions, the prophets, sects or symbols of the various religious communities; and – to protect Arab identity from the harmful effects of globalization." (cf. Al-Tahhawi, 2008)

Especially the claim to protect family values, family structure, and religious values may be perceived as an attempt to limit possible re-negotiations of gender roles and practices as well as to limit the creation of new gender spaces by new programming. Thus, the Islamic satellite television is equally morally restricted by the Islamic ideas behind the channels and by the State control. Still, how does this affect the *space* offered to the audience by the channels and how is this space becoming a morally defined space?

As the findings of the stereotypical representation of women in Arab media exemplify, television has often been analysed as mediator of representations, pictures and ideas. Television belongs to and may be examined, within what

---

1 The national Egyptian television ERTU (Egyptian Radio and Television Union) is a typical example, where the programme politics states that any programme *"touching on women's status would be prohibited from criticizing religion and traditions, 'threatening' family ties or 'disparaging' the sanctity of family values."* (Sakr, 2004b, p. 9).

Lefebvre according to Cresswell has defined as "the domain of representations and image" (Cresswell, 2002, p. 21). Compared to 'Firstspace' which is Lefebvre's term for empirically measurable and mappable phenomena, this 'Secondspace' is subjective and imagined. This distinction between a more material concept of *place* and a more abstract concept of *space* has been reconstructed in many cultural geographic studies according to Cresswell. Parallel to Lefebvre's suggestion for developing a concept of 'Thirdspace', Cresswell argues for a concept of place which in some ways combines the measurable place with the imagined place. By introducing the meaning of practical knowledge with reference to the practice theory of Pierre Bourdieu and Judith Butler's theory on gendered embodied practices, he argues that place is getting meaning and importance as *practised and lived* "rather than simply being material (conceived) or mental (perceived)" (p. 21). The practical knowledge is not only embodied, it is also *placed* in the world. The relationship between body and world is thus continuously reproduced and potentially transgressed. Body and place are always the unfinished result of a process of constant reproduction. Place provides a model for practice and practice reproduces place. Place is a stage for performance and place is performed. According to Cresswell we need to think of place "in a constant sense of becoming through practice and practical knowledge" (Cresswell, 2002, p. 26).

The approach to place (or space) as brought into being through practice appears as particularly relevant to my study of mainly four reasons. First, disagreements about how to conceptualise transnational public spheres indicate similar considerations. Many media researchers prefer the concept of transnational *spaces* to the anthropological use of transnational *social fields* (cf. Levitt & Glick-Schiller, 2004). A main argument for using transnational spaces is that using transnational media does not automatically lead to transnational social practices or identities within the globe as a shared place, but due to media practices, specific transnational spaces seem to come into existence and transgress traditional empirical and material places. In accordance with the outline for this book and as suggested by Lefebvre, I adhere to the concept of space. However, I use the concept in agreement with the suggestions of Cresswell. Space is like place brought into being due to practice. Thus, the concept of *lived space* is becoming meaningful and whenever I use the term space in the following, I am referring to *lived space*.

Second, the approach to media as a place of practice is further supported by the development within media research. The media output is not to be evaluated by the ideology of the producer only or by the message of the programme. The audience is not a passive receiver of media messages, ideology and products. Rather the audience is taking part in different media practices (Croteau & Hoynes, 1997). One is the practice of the *interpretive* activity that the audience takes part in by constructing meanings of media messages. Another is the practice of being *participants* in the programmes by taking active part, e.g. in reality shows, in phone-in programmes or as experts. This interactivity between audience and media is an increasing aspect of current media (Hoover, 2006, p. 70). The activity of interpretation is deeply *socially* embedded emphasizing the audience's engagement with media in social settings during their consumption of media or by their sharing of interpretations and experiences with media in continuation of actual use (Croteau & Hoynes, 1997; Morley, 1980). For instance, the Arab drama serials and the cinema can be analysed as offering a specific social space to the audience wherein they can confirm, reject or renegotiate the implications of the traditional woman role presented, as anthropologist Lila Abu-Lughod has argued. For instance, she demonstrates in her studies on Egyptian drama serials how differently the urban and rural audiences make use of the drama serials in their interpretation of their own life (Abu-Lughod, 1995). In order to be a participant in the programmes, one needs to have practical knowledge about the practice of the programme. The participant is expected to practice or embody the subject position offered by the programme. In continuation of Cresswell's focus on practice theory, it is possible to talk about an embodied knowledge being practised, but also negotiated, confirmed or rejected by the participants in the programme and by the audience of the programmes. Hence, both kinds of activities can be analysed as part of the audience's identity formation through meaning constructions and through socially embedded cultural and religious identifications (Hoover, 2006, p. 16 ff).

Third, the practice perspective to media and place is at the same time in accordance with the development within the study of religious identities. As Hoover is arguing, instead of understanding religion as *ascribed*, it is more meaningful to understand religion as *achieved* (Hoover, 2006, p. 39). Religious identity is (like place) a result of a never ending process of practices and identifications. Hoover refers to Wade Clark Roof, who defines it as *lived religion* (ibid., p. 55). I have thus argued for the viewpoint that it seems theoretically fruitful to explore the media as a space of lived religion.

Fourth, an empirical argument may add further support to the choice of analytical perspective. In general, the Islamic channels present themselves as promoters of a universal Islam. However, they do not specify which kind of Islam they are promoting, except for very general statements about a moderate and tolerant Islam (Galal, 2009). Obviously, Islam becomes the normative framework, but as the channels do not specify their theological or ideological position, it becomes even more inevitably to look at the practice of the programmes. Even the channels themselves seem to find it more important to offer a space for practicing and identifying with Islam than to offer a clear definition of what it means to be Muslim. The particularity of the mediated space is constructed in practice, not in theory. In order to find out how the Islamic satellite television complies with the reality of Arab women, one must therefore explore how the spaces of the programmes are brought into being.

As an overall observation, it is possible to conclude that the new transnational media has resulted in more pluralistic, but also more specialised mediated spaces than those transmitted by national TV (cf. Galal, 2009; Sakr, 2004b). The transnational reach of Arab and non-Arab media has given access to more information and more differentiated representations of Arab women. Contrary to a shared idea to address a unified Arab Muslim audience, transnational TV offers different lived spaces defined by religious, social and political differences, life style differences not least. At the same time, the spaces being transnational, they invite Muslims from all over the world to participate in the religious practices or dialogues promoted. As the spaces are very often specialised, including gendered, a large part of the programmes raise issues particularly defined as of interest to women. As for the Islamic satellite-channels, the spaces offered are religiously framed and do not as such challenge the idea of religiously founded gender roles. Instead, the programmes seem to create a space where the existing gender roles can be lived or contested on the grounds of the interpretation of Islam. The same strategy can be found within the most influential women movement in the Arab countries for the last twenty years, the so-called Islamic feminism. The Islamic feminism argues for equal rights between men and women by referring to Islamic values.

Arab and Islamic Satellite-Television

Since the first Islamic channel, *Iqraa* (Read/Recite)[2], was presented in 1998, a considerable number of Islamic and Christian Arab religious satellite channels have been launched. Especially since 9/11, the number exploded, as today about 50 Islamic and 15 Christian Arab satellite channels are being broadcasted. Islamic channels are, in my definition, channels whose main purpose is to mediate Islamic values and perspectives and hence make a religious mediated and Arabic(-language) Islamic space available to the audience. The increase in religious channels must be understood in relation to a general huge increase in Arab satellite channels. Since the introduction in 1990 of the first Arab satellite channel, the state-owned Egyptian

---

2   Iqraa is the imperative of the verb 'read' or 'recite'. The word 'read'/'recite' was the first word revealed to the Prophet Mohammed, according to Islamic belief. Today, Muslims often refer to this revelation as a reminder of the importance to Muslims to educate themselves.

Satellite Channel (ESC1), the number of Arab satellite channels has increased to at least 500.

The new Islamic satellite channels do not, unlike many Web pages and different kinds of pamphlets with more obvious sectarian affiliation, emanate from religious groups or organizations, but rather from business investors and consortia. While many of the Christian channels are launched by churches or religious leagues[3], the Islamic channels are mostly non-denominational, with Islam proclaimed as a shared value, but not declared as officially identifying with a legal school, interpretation, or creed. Thus, popular Islamic channels like *Iqraa, Al-Majd*, and *Al-Resalah*[4] are all owned by Saudi multimillionaires with close affiliations to the Saudi royal family. The religious channels are established as part of greater business empires, which might include other media and other kinds of business investments. Iqraa is an example of this tendency.

The commercial aspect in the business of Islamic satellite TV not necessarily means that the main players do not differ in religious interpretation and ideology, nor does it mean that they cannot have a political, as well as religious, aim. Obviously, the aim is to spread knowledge about Islam and to promote Islamic values and lifestyle. While the interpretation of Islam differs, the general view is that an Islamic approach exists to all aspects of life. The majority of the channels are Sunni-Muslim channels, although some have *Sufi*[5]-affiliations, and others are *Salafi*,[6] with close connections to the Saudi religious establishment. But, even Saudi-owned channels differ greatly. Al-Majd is conservative in promoting Saudi cultural practices. Whereas Iqraa is moderate – in the meaning not going to ex-

---

3 Among the Christian channels are, for example, Sat7, launched in 1996, and governed by an independent International Board where the majority of the members are elected representatives of Middle Eastern and North African Churches and ministries. Tele Lumiere (1991) and Noursat (2003) are both supervised by the Assembly of Catholic Patriarchs and Bishops in Lebanon, and are directed by a committee involving religious leaders from various denominations and a group of laity. Aghapy TV was launched in 2005 by the Coptic Orthodox Church in Egypt.

4 I have chosen to follow the channels' own transcription of their names into English.

5 In 2008, a new private channel is being launched in Egypt, defining itself as Sufi-affiliated (according to a personal interview with the BBC, 17. Dec. 2007). In a broad sense, *Sufism* can be described as the interiorization and intensification of Islamic faith and practice. However, the term Sufism has been defined in many and opposing ways, and to give an exact definition is almost impossible. The best one do, according to Chittick (1995), is to denote it "to be the living spirit of the Islamic tradition" (Chittick, 1995, p. 103). Sufism is represented by sufi orders that are social organizations and spaces for personal piety and sufi rituals.

6 *Salafi* refers to Muslim reform movements at the turn of twentieth century that aimed at renewal of Muslim life. Since then, many Muslim thinkers and movements have been inspired by the salafi ideas and have formed different schools or directions within salafism. A key issue of the renewal is to emphasize the need to return to original Islam, very often by referring to the time of the prophet and his followers (Shahin, 1995).

tremes but following the middle course (Wasatiyah). Also, to some extent, Iqraa addresses Muslims all over the world acknowledging their differences by picturing different Muslim cultural and social spaces. Al-Resalah is somewhat a mixture. By speaking the language of ordinary people and by addressing their daily problems, it strives to embrace modernity. Simultaneously, it holds on to a traditional religious text interpretation. In general, the Islamic channels do not directly or openly support any state or political movement.[7] Instead, they highlight a pious and religious lifestyle and promote specific Islamic identity policies. Instead of discussing economic and foreign politics, the channels present and discuss the lifestyle of the individual Muslim, and the moral and ethical ideals of the Muslim community. While claiming to represent a universal Islam, the interpretation might implicitly be in accordance with particular national cultural traditions, like Al-Majd. As such, the channels can be seen as politico-religious strategies for Islamic Mission (the Arab concept of *Dawa*), dominated by Saudi *Salafi* tradition.

It is important to note that the increase in Arab satellite channels parallels the development of transnational media in general. It has resulted in a growing specialization, where religious channels are just one among a range of other specializations. A range of new programming, mixing popular culture, Islam, and religious teaching, has been introduced (Galal, 2008). It is not only the religious satellite channels who broadcast religious programmes, but many of the secular satellite channels are also now broadcasting a greatly diverse range of different programmes, including religious programmes. Entertainment is the most popular genre which applies to Islamic TV as well. Concepts of entertainment are the same: quizzes, cartoons, films, life style programmes, talk shows, and so on. The religious programmes are in turn influenced by Islamic symbols, rituals, and identity positions; for example, in programmes about 'how to find a spouse in the proper Muslim way'[8] or 'how to wear your Muslim headscarf in different fashions and styles'.[9] In addition, the core ritual elements of Islam, such as Qur'an recitation, praying, and the interpretations of *halal* and *haram* (lawful and unlawful in Islam) have assumed media form (Galal, 2008 & 2009).

The Islamic satellite-channels and the Arab satellite-channels in general do represent a paradox: On the one hand, the satellite-channels in general claim to support Islamic and/or Arab values promoting a common and unified Arab Muslim

---

7   It is possible to discuss whether a channel like *al-Manar* (the lighthouse) is religious and/or political. The channel is owned by Hizbollah, and the goal is mainly political, not religious. Despite its self-description as promoting the values of sharia, Islam is seldom included in its programmes or argumentation. I am therefore not including it in the types of channels discussed and presented in this article.
8   *Shabaab 'aayz yatgawwiz* (2004-05, Young people wanting to marry) at Iqraa.
9   *Migalit al mar'a* (2001-2006, Women's magazine) at Iqraa.

space. On the other hand, the channels' global accessibility makes it obvious to the audience how they in fact promote differentiated social, religious and linguistic spaces, rather resulting in individualisation, differentiation and even fragmentation than unity. They reflect the social differences, diverse political ideologies, unequal gender politics and how far Arabic dialects are from each other. As such, they threaten the official idea of the Arab countries sharing a common standard language, cultural and religious values, and geography. This fragmentation of former non-challenged ideas of shared values might be one of the incentives behind an increasing focus on different ways of women lives. Not only does the satellite-television give voices to women on a scale never seen before, but they also present lived life which has previously been tabooed. The issues are women encountering daily violence, being imprisoned, being prostitutes, living in the middle of armed conflicts etc.[10] Also the audience is fragmented living in different areas of the world as a national majority or as an immigrant minority, as highly educated or as illiterate, as rich or poor. As far as satellite broadcast is no longer restricted to the upper class and the elite, several observers have pointed at the potential of reaching the many illiterate women in the Arab countries, who can not read the printed press (Amin, 2001). The potential for women's access to differentiated and specialised mediated spaces is enormous. However, the main obstacle might be, as Hussein Amin (2001) argues the fear of the threat against Arab culture and traditions limiting programming that threatens family ties or condemns family values. Arab state television is thus challenged by new forms of transnational television. State television has typically had the objective to construct a national public within a national and for many Arab countries secular public space. They have used, what Lila Abu-Lughod (2005) calls, national pedagogy to educate and construct the people as national citizens.

Few have until now studied the Islamic media as a space for religious practices and identification, as *lived space*. In-depth studies of religious programming seem hitherto to focus first and foremost on changes in interpretation of the Qur'an and changes of religious authority (cf. Galal, 2003; Roald, 2001; Skovgaard Petersen, 2004). These studies do only peripherally include the relationship to the audience. To explore the Islamic programming as lived space, at the same time is to take the audience seriously as participants in the interpretation and use of the programmes. Consequently, the lived space is not restricted to the media itself; rather the media provides the platform for a specific lived place. To be able to demonstrate some of the implications of the religious programming examined as lived spaces, I have chosen to consider different kinds of lived spaces promoted

---

10 Sakr (2004) mentions for instance the programme *Lil Nisaa Faqat* (For Women Only) at al-Jazeera as a programme raising controversial questions.

by the Islamic satellite-channel Iqraa. I have chosen Iqraa for different reasons. First, Iqraa is the first Islamic satellite-channel launched and has due to its initial and instant success become an exemplary model for successive channels. Second, Iqraa is the easiest accessible Islamic channel in Europe due to its transmission via the European satellite Hotbird. Hotbird is much easier to reach by satellite dish than satellites like Arabsat and Nilesat being the preferred satellites for other Arab channels.[11] After a short introduction to this channel, I will present and analyse three different lived spaces offered by Iqraa.

Islamic Programming on Iqraa

The first Arab Islamic satellite channel, Iqraa, was launched with the specific goals 1) to support the values of the Arab-Islamic Nation stressing the moderate Islamic identity, 2) to stress the fundament of al-Qur'an and al-Sunna (the example of the prophet Muhammad), 3) to protect the Arab-Islamic Nation against imported non-Islamic culture, 4) to support the relations between the different Arab countries, and 5) to produce quality entertainment programmes to the Arab family.[12] The focus of the programmes on Iqraa is stated as being 'Islamic values' without more specific definitions in addition to presenting itself as promoting moderate Islam. It broadcasts a variety of programmes, from children's programmes and talk shows, to lifestyle programmes, all with a so-called Islamic perspective.

Iqraa was launched by ART (Arab Radio and Television) being owned by Saudi multimillionaire, Salih Kamel. Today, Iqraa is one of 21 thematic commercial channels broadcasted by ART which include, for example, film, sport, cartoon, and news channels. When ART set off in 1994, the company was broadcasting from Rome, Italy, with a smaller number of channels. ART has studios in Egypt, Jordan, Saudi Arabia, and Lebanon where the programmes are also produced. Commercial stations, like ART, typically buy foreign entertainment channel programmes, rather than produce their own, but the religious programmes broadcast on Iqraa are mainly from their own production.

Iqraa presents itself as non-political and has not least gained popularity due to the use of former actresses and singers now employed as pious and hijab-dressed studio hostesses. They are the so-called 'repentant' artists or 'new-born' Muslims who have chosen Islam, serving God instead of the fascinating fame.[13] Arab

---

11 While Iqraa is transmitted via both Hotbird, Arabsat and Nilesat, Al-Resalah and Al-Majd are only available via Arabsat and Nilesat; Nilesat being difficult to receive in Northern Europe.
12 See http://www.iqraatv.com.
13 For an analysis of the 'repentant' artists, cf. van Nieuwkerk (2008).

press has written extensively about these new TV-stars. At the same time the channel is dominated by Egyptians which makes the programmes easier to understand in the different Arab countries. The dominant position of Egyptian film, music, culture as well as Egyptian migrant workers has made the Arabs more accustomed to listen to the Egyptian dialect compared with other dialects or modern standard Arabic.

Iqraa broadcasts different women programmes reflecting the most popular type of programmes in general. It is possible to distinguish between three types, offering spaces for different aspects of Muslim life: the talk shows, the fatwa programmes, and the life style programmes. There is of course a range of variations under each of these three categories, but as ideal typical programme genres they do fulfil different needs for the Muslim women. In the talk shows various topics relevant for the Arab societies are raised. What characterises the talk show is the emphasis on talking itself. *The talk show* is a space for talk and discussion and to various degrees of disagreement. In *the fatwa programmes* talking is mostly a tool to reach the aim of communicating the truth and giving answers in accordance with Islam. Within this genre, disagreement is in principle not a possible option. The fatwa programme is a space to fulfil the religious obligation of searching for true answers. *The life style programmes* are programmes covering different ways of living while focusing on individual choices and material possibilities. The aim is to facilitate and demonstrate attractive opportunities in life without compromising the Islamic values. It is a space of dreaming, consuming, and styling your life as Islamic.

In the following I will give examples from all three types of programmes as transmitted by Iqraa. Especially I will elaborate on a specific talk show named 'Before the Day of Judgement' *(Qabil an tuhaasabu*[14]*)*.

The Talk Show: Space for Dialogue and Re-Negotiation

The talk shows are typically characterised by a certain degree of interactivity and thus giving the word to women themselves through call-in programmes or by interviewing women in their own environments. Mostly, the programmes also include experts placed in the studio commenting or analysing a case.

The talk show 'Before the Day of Judgement' *(Qabil an tuhaasabu)* is a weekly programme at Iqraa broadcasted in primetime. The programme is hosted by Basma Wahba, who has the role of the insisting interviewer raising controversial questions. She is dressed according to the latest Islamic trend with coloured dress

---

14 A literal translation of the title would be: 'Before you are getting settled with'.

and hijab, the hijab being arranged in a decorative and sophisticated manner. The message of the Islamic tradition or *sharia* in relation to the specific case raised is always questioned. The programme takes up the same controversial issues as secular talk shows, for instance female prisoners. The topic of two successive programmes was girls and young women living in the street. It tells the story about women facing a life with sexual and violent abuse, several sexual relationships, drug dependence, the risk of getting a child outside marriage and recurrent arrests. Within Islam and in the Arab countries in general, not only prostitution but also getting a child outside marriage is taboo. Getting a child outside marriage is considered inappropriate and the child has limited legal rights.

The two programmes were broadcasted in September 2006.[15] The programmes tell the story of four girls, all living in the streets of Cairo. They are interviewed by the hostess who encourages them to tell their own stories with their own words. Before and after the interviews, the hostess is sitting in a garden together with different experts with specialised knowledge on the subject, commenting the specific case or discussing more principal aspects of the subject. The second programme is introduced by short crosscutting clips from the interview with the girl Aya, the statements of the experts and the voice of the hostess raising some questions. Questions such as: 'Are these girls victims or are their problems self-inflicted? Are they telling the truth or are they lying? What circumstances have forced the girl to live as she does?' During the interview, we see tears in the eyes of both the girl and the hostess. Aya asks God for forgiveness for the life she has lived, while she weeps. The hostess utters: 'God willing', and continues by asking: 'Is this from your heart?' Aya verifies passionately.

The setting is, thus, a repentant girl who not only presents her life on the street as cruel and completely destructive, but also as wrong and immoral. The programme is religiously framed. A Muslim sheikh being present among the experts is positioned by the hostess as someone who has the authority to judge the life of the girl. Nevertheless, the programme is surprisingly loyal to Aya and what she finds important for her situation. Hers is a long story of neglect from her mother, the system, especially the police and social workers, and not least from the many men exploiting the unprotected position of the abandoned girl. She is actually being given the chance to express herself on her own terms. The hostess does not interrupt her story with critical questions during the interview but does repeatedly ask the girl to explain and go more thoroughly into details about her emotions in specific situations. By giving the voice to Aya, the programme certainly breaks cultural taboos: mothers giving up their children, rape and violence towards women not only by men in the local community but also by the police, prostitution, children living in the streets, and young girls giving birth to children without know-

---

15 The first programme was sent on 18th of September, the second programme on 25th of September 2006.

ing the father. At the same time the programme unveils a society which is not capable of dealing with these matters, nor able to support the girl in pursuing a better life.

However, the programme is not only about breaking taboos. It is also about how to discuss these issues from an Islamic point of view. Hence, the programme demonstrates how Muslim women can participate in discussions on social issues. It offers a space for dialogue and negotiation including women on equal terms. One could argue that the programme unveils the hypocrisy of a society imagining itself as a society that is especially caring, a protector of family values, and respectful of women with reference to Islam. At the same time these values are of course established as the true ones by interpreting the free sexual life of these women as destructive and a reaction to extreme conditions of life. The sexual activities of the girl are a returning subject in the discussion with the experts, sometimes to correct prejudices as the common idea that women who are raped want it themselves, and sometimes to state the obvious misfortune of these girls' lives.

The experts in the programme are four men and two women; besides the Muslim sheikh, there is a psychiatrist, two social workers and two researchers. They are being questioned about how to interpret the behaviour of the girls and the practice of the State in relation to the girls. One of the main themes of the discussion is the question of the girls' guilt: "Are their problems self-inflicted?" The hostess does through the whole programme position the girls as victims for circumstances on which they have no influence. Their families let them down; the authorities let them down; and men let them down. At the same time the hostess and the girls themselves position the girls as moral individuals by presenting them as repentant. They are not presented as morally responsible, but are left with their moral integrity.

None of the experts interpret the situation as a question of personal guilt. The Muslim sheikh Higaazi, who is particularly asked by the hostess to judge the behaviour of the girl morally, is refusing to do so. He quotes Islamic theology saying that one has to judge in every single case, where all the circumstances must be considered. If a girl is under pressure, she can not be responsible. As the discussion carries on, the Doctor in psychiatry, Hashim Bahari from *al-Azhar* University, starts talking about the girls' nice appearance and their strategy for survival. The women experts seem to interpret his statements as though he is questioning whether the girls are victimized:

> **Bahari**: "Let's go back to the clip, we have just seen. My first impression is a person who has been a victim of a very violent conflict. In those situations, the girl wants to get the sympathy from other people and therefore she makes use of all means. […] In this case, it is to hide or fabricate stories or to lie; methods which children learn to protect themselves and not because they are born liars."
> **Hostess**: "You mean that what she tells is a lie?"
> **Bahari**: "I do not know what is true and what is not. […] No doubt, the girl has been taken care of. And she has been interviewed one of those places offering caring. But, if we look

closer at the first impression, we notice that she cares about her makeup. Her face shows that she takes care of herself."
Hostess: "Are we talking about the girl we just saw? She is not wearing makeup at all."
Bahari: "Yes, she has had her eyebrows done."
Hostess: "She is not wearing makeup at all."
Bahari: "It is obvious that she is taken care of herself. That is good, but it tells us how she is. It tells us that she is not completely ruined."
Al-Badri (female guest): "Yes, but this is due to the caring she is getting currently. As mentioned, we do teach them a profession. We want them to get out and work as a hairdresser, cook, or carpet weaver. So, when they are taught to become a hairdresser, they practice on each other."
Hostess: "It is true. I have seen it."

Bahari's comments are the only attempt to position the girls as more than just victims and this attempt is immediately rejected by the hostess and al-Badri.

A similar contestation occurs when the hostess asks the experts to consider the many sexual relations of the girls. Again, the sheikh is asked to present how Islam looks upon the girl having non-consensual sex. Higaazi stresses that the girl can not be judged if she has been forced to sex. In that case she is forgiven according to Islam. He differentiates between force, resignation, and voluntary consent. By indicating the possibility of consent in the cases of the presented girls, the female guest, Al-Baz, asks:

Al-Baz: "Yes, but if she is very young?".
The sheikh: "That is why I am stressing that from a religious point of view, we need as religious scholars to judge every in its own terms. Another girl would try to find a man to protect her. In her case, I do not regard it as force."
Al-Baz: "This is a very important question. Why does our society judge? (The guests speak all at once). I want an answer from *maullanaa* (our religious scholar). He must give a clear answer. Why does our society judge a sexual relationship with closed eyes? [...] the girl has been taught about sexuality under troubled circumstances and in a very young age. She has not got to know how to systematise her sexual emotions or her own relationship."
Al-Badri (female guest): "The girl has become active, *maullanaa*."
Al-Baz: "She has not learned anything. She has spontaneous emotions. They have not been mature."
The sheikh: "She might also have practiced this without knowing that it is *haram* (forbidden)."
Hostess: "Yes, that is right. She has never learned science or religion, neither what is shame or *haram*."

The conversation illustrates how the women are defending the position of the girls emphasising the direct or indirect violence involved in their sexual relations. They challenge the sheikh by requesting him to make things clear. By addressing him with the title *maullanaa*, meaning 'our religious scholar', they challenge his authority as the title is used with thick sarcasm. His retreat is obvious when he stresses that the girls might not know what they are doing.

The issue about consent or use of force is taken up again later in the conversation. The hostess refers to a popular and prejudiced conception of women inviting rape themselves. This, according to the programme's widespread conception, is rejected by everyone. However, the experts seem to address different aspects of the girls' situation. Thus, Higaazi ignores the most controversial aspects of the girl's life. For instance, he never explicitly acknowledges the part of the girl's story about the sexual or violent abuses or the prostitution. Instead, he refers to the marriage of the girl as what makes her sexual behaviour legal, ignoring that the husband obviously is mean and violent and might even work as her pimp. The only reason for the girl to marry him was to get out and away from the street. On the contrary, he talks about how the man in general should behave in a marriage according to Islam.

In general three of the men talk in a very theoretical and principal manner about the girls' situation; likewise they never use the word rape or sexual intercourse. The taboo is still prevalent and they do not offer her any way out by defining her rights. The two women experts are the ones who introduce the word 'rape' and the fourth (a younger man) is the one to present studies on the sexual and violent abuses of the police and social workers towards girls as well as boys living in the streets. The hostess talks on behalf of the girls several times during the experts' discussion, and thus becomes the loyal mouthpiece of the girls.

Not only does the programme give voices to a very marginalised and stigmatised group of women in Egypt, it also abstains from judging the women on moral-religious grounds. Instead it highlights the responsibility of the society despite the fact that the programme is broadcasted on a religious channel under the title: *Before the Day of Judgement*. Seen in the perspective of spaces brought into being by practice, the programme suggests a public space where Muslim women can take part, express their opinions, and challenge conventional taboos and prejudices. They can even challenge the religious authority and they can talk openly about sex, rape, and exploitation. And they can do so without compromising their faith. The talk show is not rejecting Islam or Islamic teaching; rather Islam seems to be an instrument to legitimise the break of taboos. To conclude, in this specific case, the talk show is a public space where women are participative citizens with equal rights to contest, negotiate, and interpret societal issues.

The Fatwa Programme: Space for Finding Religious Answers

The fatwa programme is a well known genre. The setting is simple. A Muslim scholar is answering questions from the audience about how to live a Muslim life in accordance with the Qur'an and Sunna.[16] A general concern is the dilemmas

---

16 Sunna refers to practices undertaken or approved by the Prophet and established as legally binding precedents complementing the divinely revealed message of the Qur'an. As such, Sunna becomes a source for establishing norms for Muslim conduct. Among recent researchers, Sunna is seen as a

related to living in a modern world and complying with Islamic guidelines. The fatwa programme is as genre directed at both men and women. They call in by phone, or send fax or email with their questions. It attracts Muslims from all over the world. Quite often Muslims call or email from countries of immigration asking about how to comply with living in a non-Muslim society while trying to fulfil the obligations of a Muslim. On Iqraa there are several programmes which can be categorized as fatwa-programmes, of which some are directed specifically towards women as far as they raise questions on the Muslim woman and her life from a Muslim perspective. In the programmes there are religious experts – women or men – to answer the viewer's questions. Let me give a few examples.

The programme "Fatwas for women" (*Fatwa an-Nisaa*) is a weekly programme discussing a new subject every time. In September 2006 the topic was about women's economical rights during and after a marriage.[17] The programme stated the right of women to work; that she has the right to save the money for herself, because the husband according to Islam is the breadwinner, and that she – if she wants to – might support the family economy with her income. The programme ended up saying that economically the Muslim woman has more rights than the man. Another example is a programme from July 2005[18] called "The Islamic Jurisprudence of Women" (*Fiqh in-Nisaa*). The programme illustrates a popular topic in the Islamic programmes. It focused on and argued for agreement within an Islamic and scientific view on life. Instead of perceiving the two perspectives as opposite, we should regard them as complementing each other. The subjects were bleeding after giving birth, menstruation bleedings of the women in general, and the condition of the womb after giving birth. They are all subjects which according to the logic of the argument already have been uncovered by Islam but have since then been proved right by modern science as well.

First, these examples demonstrates how the programme within an Islamic framework takes up women's rights, the question of gender equality, and also promotes a discourse where women's biological functions and problems can be discussed openly. Once again, the Islamic framework of the programme gives it legitimacy without compromising the faith. Hence, and secondly, the programme offers a space for a European audience to take up discussions of modernity and Islam, human and gender rights within Islam and at the same time find a way to include it in an Islamic religious discourse. Thirdly, and maybe of most interest in connection with space brought into being, is the ritualistic use of the fatwa

---

multivalent concept serving as a common template for different Muslims groups and individuals, "permitting them to represent a connection with the beginnings of Islam and acting as a common referent in the religious discourse of community formation and identity". (Nanji, 1995, p. 137).
17 Fatawi an-Nisaa – Fatawi ramadaaniya 2006-09-23.
18 2005-07-13 Fiqh in-Nisaa at Iqraa.

programmes. They are not only a room for getting answers. They are also being constructed as a space wherein Muslims, placed all over the world, can take part in the same religious ritual at the same time; the ritual of jihad in the understanding of striving for truth. The ritual activity is constructing and performing a specific relationship between the human beings and an authority or power outside the normal reach of the humans, thereby letting people embody and implement their positions in a higher order (Bell, 1997: xi). Thus, the continuous repetition of the same questions has a ritualistic function confirming the relationship to God and the moral order of Islam. Those are questions of gender relations, the headscarf, alcohol, where and how to pray under exceptional circumstances, the issue when job conditions forces the Muslim to break Islamic rules etc. By calling in to ask these questions, the believer is not only demonstrating that he or she is taking Islam seriously, the person in question is actually practising and performing Islam by participating in the programme, regardless of whether the call is done in person or by substitute. The fatwa programme becomes what Cresswell calls "an unstable stage for performance" (Cresswell 2002, p. 25). By the repetition of act – passing on questions – the meaning are never finally fixed, as Cresswell writes (Cresswell 2002, p. 22). Rather, it is the repetition of act which brings the religious identity and space into being and not a once and for all definition.

The Life Style Programme: Space for Consumption and Identification

The third kind of programme is the life style programme. It is a broad concept including programmes on cooking, fashion, health and programmes on family life, marriage and child raring. The life style programme mirrors the women programmes in general, raising questions related to modern lifestyle and at the same time defending basic traditional values. Thus, it is never questioned that sex before marriage is wrong. Neither is it challenged that the foundation of the family is moral values and religion. The right partner is therefore first and foremost a believing and religious practicing Muslim, who knows his or her religion and serves God. A programme raising these questions is "Youngsters wanting to get married" (*shabaab 'aayz yatgawwiz*)[19], being a weekly programme. The experts in the studio have either religious or secular educational background, and in between the discussions of the experts, people in the streets are asked about their opinion or experience in relation to a certain topic. The atmosphere of the programme is presented as very relaxed with a lot of joking and laughing among the experts as they were sitting at home in their living rooms. This atmosphere is emphasized

---

19 2005-09-17 at Iqraa.

by the scenery, where the guests are placed in two sofas with the hostess in the middle in what seems to be a very modern living room. The number of women guests normally outdoes the number of men, and we might imagine a daily life gathering among women discussing the usual women topics. As such the show invites the female audience, sitting in any country, to take part in an imagined social setting where intimate issues, partly related to the private sphere, are discussed within an Islamic framework. Simultaneously, the issues raised are mostly related to private spaces of family and home. Thus, the programme promotes a religious performance of Muslim women and in so doing brings another lived space into being: the private space. Consequently, the private lived space encouraged is strongly normative despite its focus on consumption and well-being.

Dilemmas of wanting to live a modern life while fulfilling religious obligations are often addressed by rejecting traditional elements of Arab and Muslim traditions. For instance, the programme regularly contests the traditional practices where the parents choose the spouse or where the size of the *mahr* (dowry) is more important than the feelings between the future wife and husband. The programme states that it is important to listen to one's parents but the parents should also listen to and understand young people and what is important to them in society today. The *mahr* has to be reasonable and one should not demand big flats or expensive furniture. By exchanging tradition with Islam, the programmes do also meet the dilemmas of young Muslims living in European countries. Instead of following the tradition of their parents, they are offered a space where Islam and not specific national or local traditions are presented as the common denominator.

Life style programmes about Islamic fashion, decorating your house in an Islamic fashion, cooking or doing sport are other prevalent programmes. They mostly address the middle and upper classes by giving examples from practices and lifestyle unattainable for poor women and in general very far from the practices of lower classes in any Arab country. On the other hand, they offer a space for the immigrant women living in Western societies in where they can practice living in a modern consumer society without compromising Islam. They are offered a space where they can consume the Islamic way. A Muslim pious consumer and lived space is brought into being.

Spaces for Religious and Gendered Performance

I introduced this paper by referring to the moral obligations raised by the receiving immigrant countries towards the Muslim woman. These are moral obligations with the purpose of complying with values of gender equality as defined by the European countries. I have tried do demonstrate how the Islamic satellite-channels do offer spaces where the Muslim immigrant women can negotiate these moral obligations and at the same time live up to another important set of moral obligations defined within Islam. The programmes I have analysed seem to offer different kinds of participative spaces in which Muslim women can take part as audience or by calling in. The talk show provides spaces for discussion and negotiation where the Muslim woman can participate as a citizen with her specific experiences and knowledge. Compared to similar public discussions available in a European majority setting, the Islamic programmes do make it possible to raise controversial issues within a traditional Islamic framework. Thus, the Muslim woman is given the opportunity to negotiate her double belonging simultaneously. A similar point could be concluded regarding the fatwa programmes. They offer the Muslim audience a space for the participative believer. This space is not only an educational space but an alternative ritualistic space to the mosque or organisation. Once again, the Islamic channels promote space which in its self-understanding is universal and freed of local traditions. Seen from the immigrant women's perspectives, it might be attractive as an alternative religious space because it is not left to the local religious authority to regulate her behaviour. It is first and foremost her individual choice to comply with the answers given by the mediated fatwa. As for the life style programmes, they offer the audience a space to participate in consumption of different kinds but all defined as in accordance with Islam.

Linda Khatib argues in her article *The Orient and its Others* that the representation of the Islamic fundamentalist in Egyptian cinema presents the Islamist woman as either an example of the moral depravity of Islamist militancy or as the image of the silent, veiled woman to symbolize its oppressiveness (Khatib, 2004, p. 73). The representation of the Muslim woman in the women programmes at Iqraa is much more complex offering spaces for different kinds of participative lives. Also, the performative spaces brought into being by the programming are plural and include public political, religious practising, as well as private spaces. At the same time the identity of the women presented is Islamic. This is what frames the woman as a good mother, a good wife, a clever student or professional worker. Any practice of the modern Muslim woman is evaluated on the basis of right Islamic behaviour and the way to become a Muslim is through practice. One could say that the programmes reflect an adaptation to modern life without giving up the moral order, where sexuality is in firm control and family a basic unity of society. Islam is at the same time legitimising the new life style of the women. What is never questioned, is the justice of Islam. The interpretations of Islam might be challenged and criticised, but as a righteous foundation Islam is not to be questioned. This pattern of religious, moral and social discourse is indeed prevalent in Iqraa´s programmes. An objection or moderation must end the argument. Before being too celebrative, however, it is important to emphasise that just as well as the Islamic channels might offer inclusive spaces making it possible to combine European and Muslim living, there are of course other programmes being much more exclusionary. Also, the new Islamic channels could be said to be a tool to an Islamic colonization of lived space, as far as the basis of the order of this space is unquestionably Islam. However, seen from the perspective of lived spaces, the Islamic channels by promoting particular gendered and religious spaces offer the Muslim woman spaces for performing not only religious or gender identity, but also identities transgressing division between private and public, modern and traditional, religious and civic.

References

Abu-Lughod, L. (2005). *Dramas of Nationhood. The Politics of Television in Egypt.* Cairo: The American University in Cairo Press.

–, (1995). The Objects of Soap Opera: Egyptian Television and the Cultural Politics of Modernity. In D. Miller (ed.), *Worlds Apart.* London: Routledge.

Amin, H. (2001). Arab Women and Satellite Broadcasting. *TBS*, No. 6, Spring/Summer 2001. Retrieved from http://www.tbsjournal.com/Archives/Spring01/Amin2.html

–, (2008). Arab Media Audience Research: Developments and Constraints. In K. Hafez (ed.), *Arab Media: Power and Weakness* (pp. 69-90). New York and London: Continuum.

Andreassen, R (2005). *The Mass Media's Construction of Gender, Race, Sexuality and Nationality: An Analysis of the Danish Media's Communication about Visible Minorities.* Unpublished PhD-thesis: University of Toronto.

Bell, C. (1997). *Ritual. Perspectives and Dimensions.* Oxford: Oxford University Press.

Chittick, C. C. (1995). Sufism. In J. L. Esposito (ed.), *The Oxford Encyclopedia of the Modern Islamic World.* New York & Oxford: Oxford University Press.

Cresswell, T. (2002). Introduction: Theorizing Place. In G. Verstraete & T. Cresswell (eds.), *Mobilizing Place, Placing Mobility: The Politics of Representation in a Globalized World* (pp. 11-31). Thamyris/Intersecting 9. Editions Rodopi B.V.

Croteau, D. & W. Hoynes (1997). *Media/Society: Industries, Images, and Audiences.* London: Pine Forge Press.

Galal, E. (2003). Islam via satellit. In L. P. Galal & I. Liengård (eds.), *At være muslim i Danmark* (pp. 93-107). København: Forlaget Anis.

–, (2008a). Magic Spells and Recitation-Competitions. Religion as Entertainment on Arab Satellite-Television. In S. Hjarvard (ed.), *Enchantment, Media and Popular Culture. The Mediatization of Religion.* Northern Lights.

–, (2009). *Identiteter og livsstil på islamisk satellit-tv. En indholdsanalyse af udvalgte programmers positioneringer af muslimer* (Identity and Lifestyle on Islamic Satellite-television: A content analysis of selected programmes' positioning of Muslims). PhD-thesis, Faculty of Humanities, University of Copenhagen.

Hoover, S. M. (2006). *Religion in the Media Age.* London and New York: Routledge.

Khatib, L. (2004). The Orient and its Others: Women as Tools of Nationalism in Egyptian Political Cinema. In Sakr, N. (ed.), *Women and Media in the Middle East. Power Through Self-Expression.* London, New York: I.B. Tauris.

Krag, H. (2007). *Mangfoldighed, magt og minoriteter. En introduktion til minoritets-forskningens teorier.* København: Forlaget Samfundslitteratur.

Levitt, P. & N. Glick-Schiller (2004). Conceptualizing Simultaneity: A Transnational Social Field Perspective on Society. *The International Migration Review,* Fall, 38(3): 1002-1039.

Martín-Barbero, J. (1997). Mass Media as Site of Resacralization of Contemporary Cultures. In S. M. Hoover & K. Lundby (eds.), *Rethinking Media, Religion, and Culture* (pp. 102-116). London: Sage Publications.

Morley, D. (1980). *The 'Nationwide' Audience: Structure and Decoding.* London: British Film Institute.

Murdock, G. (1997). The Re-Enchantment of the World: Religion and the Transformations of Modernity. In S. M. Hoover & K. Lundby (eds.), *Rethinking Media, Religion, and Culture.* London: Sage Publications.

Nanji, A. A. (1995). Sunnah. In J. L. Esposito (ed.), *The Oxford Encyclopedia of the Modern Islamic World.* New York & Oxford: Oxford University Press.

van Nieuwkerk, K. (2008). 'Repentant' Artists in Egypt: Debating Gender, Performing Arts and Religion. *Contemporary Islam,* 2: 191-210.

El-Omar, M. (2006). The Social Image of Women in Syrian Drama. Unpublished Paper Presented at the Conference "Woman in Syria Today". Damascus University, June 2006.

Ramzi, N. (2004). *Al maraa wa al Ilaam fi aalam mutaghayr* (The Woman and the Media in a Changing World). Maktabit al-Usra.

Sakr, N. (ed.) (2004a). *Women and Media in the Middle East. Power through Self-Expression.* London, New York: I.B. Tauris.

–, (2004b). Women-Media Interaction in the Middle East: An Introductory Overview. In N. Sakr (ed.), *Women and Media in the Middle East. Power Through Self-Expression.* London, New York: I.B. Tauris.

Shahin, E. E. (1995). Salafiyah. In J. L. Esposito (ed.), *The Oxford Encyclopedia of the Modern Islamic World.* New York & Oxford: Oxford University Press.

Al-Tahhawi, A. (2008). Arab Ministers Finally Agree – on Limiting Press Freedom. *Menassat*, 15. February 2008. Retrieved from http://www.menassat.com/?q=en/ news-articles/2968-arab-ministers-finally-agree-limiting-press-freedom.

The Exclusion of Denizens within the Irish Social and Political Opportunity Structure: The Cosmopolitan Case of Muslims in the Republic of Ireland

Des Delaney and Francesco Cavatorta

Introduction

The aim of this paper will be to analyse the social and political opportunity structures available to the Muslim population domiciled within the Republic of Ireland (ROI) and to assess how the incentives and disincentives of these structures impact on the individual choice selection of either a national or transnational identity. Critical stress will be placed on the role of the nation state for designing political structures that are exclusionary, as compared to the more open and accessible civil and social opportunities that exist. Notably, the political opportunity structure is recognised as exclusionary by the identification of a civic stratification of the Muslim community into citizens and denizens. This exclusionary institutional system is designed and perpetuated by the Irish nation state. The paper will then move onto a critical analysis of these political exclusionary structures within the Irish political community with particular emphasis on cosmopolitan theory, which aims to transcend the a-moral norms of the existing Westphalian state system and to create new modalities of dialogic communities that stop exclusion and civic stratification and enable denizens to enter the national political realm.

Firstly, the chapter provides background information on the Muslim population in the Republic of Ireland, which has been relatively ignored in European Muslim studies. Such limited research of the Irish context has been perpetuated by a relatively small population of domiciled Muslims and a continuing lack of qualitative and quantitative data that may form the basis of much needed academic insight. Due to these limitations, this paper has had to make some reluctant trade-offs. Specifically, in accordance with research conducted by Koopmans and Statham into civic pluralist polities[1] (of which the ROI has been categorised below),

---

1 Koopmans and Statham (2001) have stated within their content analysis studies on migrant claims-making that: 'inclusive citizenship regimes direct migrant identities away from the national and ethnic cleavages of their homelands' (p.93) and towards a Muslim identity. We will deal more comprehensively with this topic of political opportunity structures below.

the heterogeneous Muslim community will not be assessed according to its ethnic cleavages but as a holistic entity. Certainly, in time with continuing research and more accessible data, narrowing the focus to Muslim ethnic cleavages will be an academic priority for the Irish Muslim-studies field.

Secondly, the chapter will discuss the Irish social and political opportunity structures such as the political system; racism within Irish society; naturalisation and electoral franchise; and the educational system. The political and social opportunity structure has not been narrowed to the Muslim context *per se* but has been developed in a broad manner that may be inferred onto all migrants and third country nationals living within the Irish state. Muslim reactions to these structures have been presented through the limited academic work that exists, official organisational documents and newspaper coverage from the Irish Times, the most influential broadsheet in the country. As mentioned, the data available remains sparse in terms of European research already presented in this academic field and this chapter begins to fill this gap.

Lastly, the paper will narrow its focus on one preeminent form of exclusion identified from the social and political opportunity structure: that of the exclusion of denizens to vote in national elections within the Republic of Ireland. This exclusionary practice will be critically analysed using a cosmopolitan perspective that will emphasize the moral rigidity of the nation state system in identifying new ways of incorporating political communities that have national and transnational links. Particular emphasis will be placed on the cosmopolitan theories of Andrew Linklater and on the dialogic ethics of Jürgen Habermas.

Background to the Muslim Community in Ireland[2]

Demographically, at present, the Muslim population of the Republic of Ireland is officially calculated at 32,539, which represents an increase of 69.9 percent in the Muslim population since the previous census of 2002. This population has a male-female division of 19,372 and 13,167 respectively and is considerably young in age with 9,979 aged between 1-14; 10,140 aged between 15-29; 11,993 aged between 30-59 and lastly, 427 aged between 60-85 plus.[3]

It must be recognised that the Muslim population within the R.O.I. is extremely heterogeneous, containing over fifty different nationalities and incorporating regional links to Europe, (South) Asia, Africa, and the Middle East. Sunni sects predominate, whilst two thousand Shia are also represented[4]. In parallel

---

2 The primary reference to this section unless otherwise stated is Flynn (2006).
3 For the above statistics, see Central Statistics Office (CSO, 2010).
4 See www.shiamusliminireland.com, Retrieved on 7th November 2009.

with other European countries, immigration to the ROI was initiated due to economic and professional necessity. However, in contrast to the European experience, the first migrants to Ireland were medical students, practicing doctors, aircraft mechanics and businessmen. Muslims are well-represented in occupations in the health, sales and personal care/child care areas. In terms of geographical spread within Ireland, the census figures of 2006 indicates a balance between Dublin (17,330 pop.) and non-Dublin (15,209 pop.). Moreover, outside Dublin, the Muslim population has a tendency to reside in regional city locations or towns with populations over 5000.[5]

Notably, Muslim communities have developed in towns that contain economic resources that fit general Muslim occupational trends. For example, Cavan town has a Muslim population of 252, who benefit from a close proximity to a hospital that provides medical services for the wider provincial area. Also, in county Kerry, the small town of Tralee has a significant Muslim population of 522, who avail of the important tourist industry in which the sales and services markets thrive. The county newspaper of Kerry published an article on the Muslim population increase by stating that 'in the county capital Islam has overtaken Protestantism to become the second most practised religion in the town'.[6] Interestingly, not all economic migration within Ireland has been guided by pre-existing national determinants such as medical needs and tourism. In County Mayo, the town of Ballyhuanis has, for a thirty year period, encouraged the continued operation of a halal meat slaughtering plant, which provided halal meat to the global Muslim market. Prior to the first Gulf war and subsequent economic sanctions, the United Meat Packers (UMP) firm in Ballyhuanis was the second largest meat-processing firm in the country providing halal meat to the Middle Eastern market, particularly Saddam Hussein's Iraq. UMP was established by Pakistani entrepreneur Sher Mohammed Rafique and employed the majority of the Muslim population in the town; however, due to economic embargoes the company lost its profitability and eventually closed down. Today, a new company called Iman Casings in Ballyhuanis processes lamb casings and employs the Muslims in the town, which now stand at 146 individuals.[7]

Historically, the Republic of Ireland's Muslim community traces its origins back to the late 1950s, when a small group of students attending the Royal College of Surgeons Dublin, established a committee to organise religious needs for the

---

5   For the above statistics, see Central Statistics Office (CSO, 2010).
6   See 'Muslim Population in Kerry Doubles in Four Years' .*The Kerryman.* 5th December 2007. Available from www.kerryman.ie.
7   See 'Entrepreneur Returns to Help Mayo's Muslims' 24th July 2004 & 'Immigration has benefited Ballyhuanis' 16th May 2000. *The Irish Times.* Available from www.irishtimes.com/search/index.html

Muslim holidays and weekly Friday prayers (Arabic: *Jumaa*). From 1969 to 1976, after national and international fundraising, this expanding community established the first Islamic centre in the R.O.I, located in the South Dublin city centre. However, by 1983, with the continued expansion of the Muslim community, the Harrington Street premises was sold and personal and international donations[8] were utilised in order to buy a larger property at nearby 163 South Circular Road. Since then, this has become the home of the Dublin City Mosque along with the Islamic Foundation of Ireland (IFI). The foundation's registered members elect a new Council (Arabic: *Majlis al-Shura*) annually and it abides by a written constitution. Sheikh Yayha al-Hussein has presided as imam of Dublin City Mosque since the move to the South Circular Road.

From the early 1990s onwards, the Muslim population in the Republic of Ireland increased dramatically due to influx of refugees from Bosnia, Somalia and Albania who were fleeing their war-torn countries. In addition, by the end of the decade, there was a substantial increase in asylum seeker applications from a number of countries in Africa and the Middle East.[9] This increase in the Muslim population brought with it issues relating to physical and religious space (i.e. the limits of space within existing mosques, the lack of Islamic education and facilities outside of the Dublin metropolitan area). In November 1996, the second purpose built mosque in the R.O.I,[10] the Islamic Cultural Centre of Ireland (ICCI), was officially opened with the President of Ireland, Mary McAleese, in attendance. This large purpose built mosque, located in the middle class Dublin suburb of Clonskeagh, was initially administered by the IFI but was subsequently then managed by the Al-Maktoum Foundation, which is closely linked to and receives funding from authorities in the United Arab Emirates. The switching of administrative responsibilities from the IFI to the Al-Maktoum foundation has caused a certain amount of friction between individuals within the two organisations. Since the 1990s, advances have been made in opening and increasing the space available for the Muslim community not only in Dublin but throughout the island. At present in Dublin, there are three large mosques[11] and approximately eight prayer halls varying in size. Four of those prayer halls are located on university campuses. In the rest of Ireland, there at least 16 designated small

---

8   Donations were received from the Qatari and Kuwaiti authorities.
9   Islam in Dublin. (2010). *Islam and Muslims in Ireland*. Retrieved on 15th October, 2009. Available from www.muslimtents.com/islamindublin/ireland/htm.
10 In 1987, the Ballyhuanis Mosque became the first purpose built mosque in the Republic of Ireland.
11 The second purpose built mosque in Dublin is the Ahlul Bayt Islamic Centre [Hussainia], Milltown Bridge Dublin 14.

mosques and prayer halls. Notably, the mosques are located in the major towns and cities of each province.[12]

Social and Political Opportunity Structure

Rainer Baubock (2006) defined the political and social opportunity structure as consisting of 'laws that allocate different statuses and rights to various groups of migrants and formally constrain or enable their activities, of institutions of government and public administration in which migrants are or are not represented, of public policies that address migrants claims, concerns and interests or do not, and of a public culture that is inclusive and accepts diversity or that supports national homogeneity and a myth of shared ancestry' (p. 10). Furthermore, Baubock presents the reason behind analysing these structures. He states that 'the point of analysing a political [and social] opportunity structure is to identify institutional incentives and disincentives that help to explain migrant choices of political strategies' (2006, p. 11). This framework is helpful in outlining broad advantages and disadvantages for the domiciled Muslim community and in identifying exclusionary practices that may affect the selection of a national or transnational identity.

Irish Political System and the Absence of a Right-Wing Party

Academically, the Irish parliamentary system has been categorised as *sui generis* in composition and very much counter to the systems that exist in the rest of Europe. The Irish political system is comprised of two centre-right nationalist (republican) parties, Fianna Fail and Fine Gael, followed by a centrist Labour Party[13] and smaller left of centre political groupings such as Sinn Fein and the Green Party. The populist political strategies of the Fianna Fail Party have secured its clear domination of the political landscape since its formation in 1927, while the proportional representational (PR-STV)[14] electoral system allows for the smaller parties to maintain some form of competition and even participate in government as part of a coalition arrangement.

---

12 For a list of mosques in the Republic of Ireland, refer to www.islaminireland.com/irish_mosques.html.
13 Arguably, the Labour Party may be categorised as 'centrist' due to its social conservatism and lack of general support within the working class itself.
14 Importantly, Kingsley (1996) has recognised the limited potential within the proportional representational system for electoral block voting (a political strategy deployed by geographically concentrated Muslims in the United Kingdom) which limits the 'political potential' of settlers 'should they seek to act in unity' (pp. 129-142).

Uniquely and in contrast to most of the European political landscape today, the Irish political system is devoid of any radical right (RR) party such as has been identified in the United Kingdom (UK) with the British National Party (BNP), in France with the Front National (NF) or in Denmark with the Danish People's Party (Danish: *Dansk Folkeparti, DF*). These right-wing parties have promoted, with varying success, xenophobic immigration policies and challenged the pre-existing political consensus. Moreover, of growing concern is the increase in anti-Muslim rhetoric emanating from parties like the Danish People's Party (Rydgen, 2004). Certainly, the absence of a RR party within the Irish political system creates a more positive social and political space in which the Muslim community can participate without the added psychological and physical barriers that right-wing elements try to promote and enforce. Academics, such as Garner and O'Malley, have sought to explain this unique absence of right wing influence. Although a number of factors are outlined to account for this, most academics attribute this characteristic to the nationalist ideology that permeates the Irish political system. For example, Garner (2007) states that the norms of the Irish political system 'are not those of the European mainstream [but are in fact]...populist and nationalist' (p.114). Furthermore, O'Malley (2008) emphasises the unique populist character of Irish nationalism by stating that 'nationalism in Ireland cannot easily sit with anti-immigrant bigotry, so it is less likely that a nationalist party in Ireland could be xenophobic' (p.974). Such explanations are convincing, but should be supplemented by referring to the Proclamation of the Irish Republic[15] (Irish: *Poblacht Na hEireann*), which articulates the viewpoints of the founding fathers of the state and was signed by the leaders of the 1916 Easter Rising against British colonial rule. Notably, this document guarantees religious and civil rights and also emphasises the need for the equalisation of the enforced colonial barriers of divide and rule. The third and fourth paragraphs proclaim:

> 'The Irish Republic is entitled to, and hereby claims, the allegiance of every Irishman and Irishwoman. The Republic guarantees religious and civil liberties, equal rights and equal opportunities to all its citizens, and declares its resolve to pursue the happiness and prosperity of the whole nation and of all its parts, cherishing all the children of the nation equally, and oblivious of the differences carefully fostered by an alien government, which have divided a minority from the majority in the past.

---

15 We would contend that although the Proclamation of the Irish Republic is not an official document with legal standing within modern Ireland, its historical significance has moral and psychological resonance for the Irish nation at a collective and individual level. In a similar fashion to *liberté, égalité, fraternité* in France. However, it is a fact that a large percentage of Protestant families and individuals left Ireland after Independence. Certainly, Soysal (1994) has highlighted a term coined by Stephen Leibfried: 'There is always an '*implementation deficit*', a discrepancy between formal rights and their praxis' (p. 134).

> Until our arms have brought the opportune moment for the establishment of a permanent National Government representative of the whole of Ireland and elected by the suffrages of all her men and women, the Provisional Government, hereby constitute, will administer the civil and military affairs of the Republic in trust for the people'.[16]

Certainly, within its historical context, paragraph three of the Proclamation of Independence may be interpreted as guaranteeing a republican freedom to a homogenous entity (the Irish people) and to a certain extent appeasing and including protestant elements within Irish society. Notably, the Irish flag signifies this appeasement to the Protestant minority religion of the time (the colours green and orange linked by the white middle indicating peace between the Catholic majority and Protestant minority). Presently, in the context of a multicultural Ireland with an expanding Muslim population, the Proclamation of 1916 still proclaims religious and civil rights for all the people of Ireland, whether of a majority or minority group. It also highlights Ireland's strong opposition to colonialism's divide and rule policy, which manifested a religious divide in Ireland between Catholics and Protestants.[17] Returning to the absence of a right-wing party in the Irish political system, it must be recognised that all of Ireland's present political parties (except the Green Party) trace their political roots back to the Proclamation of Independence and its political prescriptions. That is not to say that a RR party can never exist within the Irish political arena, but that the political environment originally cast by the 1916 Proclamation makes the evolution and acceptance of such parties much more difficult.

Racism in Ireland

Although the social and political opportunity structure is positively uplifted by the absence of a RR party within the Irish political system, as in other European countries, racism still continues to affect the Muslim and other ethnic communities in Ireland. The National Consultative Committee on Racism and Interculturalism (NCCRI), in its role as the Irish National Focus Point (NFP) for the European Monitoring Centre on Racism and Xenophobia (EUMC), provides detailed six monthly reports on racist incidents which have occurred and were reported in the ROI Notably, after the plane attacks on New York, NCCRI and the Equality Authority (2001) reported that at least 'one fifth (20%) of all 41 incidents recorded between

---

16 Proclamation of the Irish Republic (*Poblacht Na hEireann*), 24th April 1916. Available from http://www.libraryireland.com/HullHistory/Appendix3b.php.
17 Notably for the last 27 years, the Republic of Ireland has annually sponsored a United Nations (U.N.) resolution condemning religious intolerance. See 'Israel to block Irish U.N. religion motion'. *The Irish Times*, 12th December 2003. Available from www.irishtimes.com/search/index.html.

May and October 2001, [were] directly related to September 11th'. The report highlights the nature of the racist attacks as unorganised acts such as abusive phone calls to mosques, verbal insults directed at Muslim women in Islamic dress and sensationalist newspaper and media reporting, which verge on being categorised as stereotypical and racist. Since 2001, the NCCRI has continued to document racist incidents within Ireland. In 2005, 119 racist incidents were reported, followed by 65 in 2006, 54 in 2007 and rising again to 106 in 2008 (NCCRI, 2005-2008). Due to recessionary times, since the end of 2008, the Irish government has decided to stop funding the NCCRI and to end the National Action Plan against Racism. Philip Watt, director of the NCCRI, publically criticised such cutbacks by stating that there is now a 'significant vacuum in Government policy arising from the fact that there is no longer an expert body to advise on anti-racism and integration and no longer a dedicated plan and funding line focused on dealing with these issues'.[18] Certainly, such cutbacks in expert monitoring of racist incidents in the R.O.I. may have a detrimental effect on the development of the Muslim communities social and political opportunity structure in the future.

Naturalisation, the Electoral Franchise and Political Participation

Political integration is another important element of the social and political opportunity structure in that 'it refers to access to political status, rights opportunities and representation for immigrants and an equalisation of these conditions between native and immigrant populations' (Baubock, 2006, p.11). It essentially analyses the level of structural integration of a given community. Naturalisation and voting franchise rights vary significantly within the European community and are still determined by the individual member states own particular policies towards political inclusion for citizens and third country nationals. The Republic of Ireland has accommodating and inclusive policies concerning naturalisation and the franchise to vote compared to other European member states. Notably, in Ireland, a minimum residence of four years is required for naturalisation with a toleration of dual nationality accepted under certain conditions.[19]

In terms of the political opportunity structure, Koopmans and Statham's (2000, 2001) content analysis work on migrant claims-making, led to the development of four ideal-typical national models of citizenship and incorporation. The model

---

18 See 'Budget Cutbacks Weaken State's Capacity to Combat Racism'. *The Irish Times*, 19th November 2008. Available from www.irishtimes.com/search/index.html.
19 See Waldrauch H. Annex – Table 1: Acquisition of nationality at birth and by naturalization in Western Europe (15 old E.U. member states, Norway and Switzerland. In Baubock (2006, pp. 106-107).

combined two citizenship elements, firstly, Brubaker's (1992) conception of *ius sanguinis*, which refers to an ethno-cultural community based on common descent and cultural traditions and *ius soli*, which refers to a civic community adhering to common political values (and institutions) and residence within the state territory. The second element concerns the state's particular cultural obligations and strategy for including migrants into the political community. Two strategies are identified: assimilationist and cultural pluralist. Assimilationism refers to a public sphere that requires new members of the political community to conform and convert to the dominant national culture. On the contrary, within cultural pluralist receiving states migrants have the right to retain their ethnic, cultural and religious differences. By combining these two elements of citizenship, Koopmans and Statham (2000, 2001) developed four ideal-typical national models of citizenship and incorporation – these are: ethnic segregationism, ethnic assimilationism, civic republicanism and civic pluralism. These distinct types of citizenship and incorporation can facilitate the identification of the two-way relationship between European state and its migrant population. Ethnic segregation has been best exemplified by Germany, which has in the past pursued policies that make it difficult for guestworkers and foreigners to naturalise and enter the political community. Therefore, *Ius sanguinis* naturalisation was applicable. However, by 2000, with the introduction of new citizenship laws, Germany made a radical transition from ethno-cultural segregationism to assimilationism. This has put more emphasis on the need for migrants (who are legally capable of naturalising) to assimilate fundamentally into the dominant German culture. In fact, Minkenberg (2003) has declared that Germany now has one of the most liberal nationality laws in Europe, by accommodating conditional *ius soli* provision and carrying out 150,000 naturalisations per year.

Civic republicanism is best exemplified by France, which has an open access to citizenship through *ius soli* but whose public sphere ascribes to a universal cultural model that does not recognise ethno-cultural groups as public entities. In fact '*communautarisme*' is reviled in French political culture.[20] Lastly, civic pluralism is identified with countries such as Sweden, the Netherlands and the United Kingdom. Like France, this type has an open access to citizenship through *ius soli*, but contra to the civic republican type recognises the cultural differences and the expression of that cultural identity in the public sphere. Notably, differences exist between the Netherlands and the U.K, in that the Netherlands has been identified as more multicultural by giving religious and ethnic groups state support for their organisations and education. This stance is related to the Pillar system (Dutch: *zuilenstelsel*) that

---

20 See 'Maverick for whom France is one and divisible'. *The Irish Times*, 23rd September 2000. Available from www.irishtimes.com/search/index.html.

has historically existed within the Dutch society.[21] However, in recent times, there are signs that the Netherlands may be moving to a more assimilationist approach by introducing naturalisation tests in culture, history and language. According to Koopmans and Statham (2000; 2001), the UK's relationship to its migrant population has in effect been racialised by a 'state-sponsored race relation industry' which has categorised sections of the migrant population as 'black' or 'Asian'. Interestingly, unlike German Muslim migrants who make claims via their ethnic affiliation, Muslim migrant claims-making in the Netherlands and the UK, is overwhelmingly presented through a 'Muslim' identity. Within the UK, this is all the more pronounced by the fact that Race Relations Act 1976 does not cover religious discrimination. As Koopmans and Statham (2001) succinctly state:

> 'inclusive citizenship regime[s] such as those of Britain and Netherlands not only affect the degree to which identity groups make homeland-oriented claims, but shape the very identities of these groups. As a result, Turks, Moroccans, or Pakistani in the Netherlands and Britain to an important extent are no longer visible in the public sphere a such, but appear as Muslims, general speakers for minorities, or, in the British Case, as representatives of the racial group of Asians [... thus] inclusive citizenship regimes direct migrant identities away from the national and ethnic categories of their homelands' (p. 93).

In relation to the Irish context, *ius soli* citizenship rights, although not automatically conferred since the Citizenship referendum in 2004,[22] are given to the second generation if one parent is resident in the state for at least three years. To acquire citizenship through marriage, an individual must by resident in the state for two years and have been married to an Irish citizen for at least three years (Baubock, 2006).[23] In terms of placement of Koopmans and Statham's typology of citizenship and incorporation, the ROI would be placed in the civic pluralist camp in between the Netherlands and the United Kingdom. In other words, within the ROI there is an open access to citizenship through *ius soli* and recognition of the cultural differences that exist within society and an acceptance of the expression of cultural and religious identity in the public sphere. In contrast to the UK and similar to the Netherlands, Ireland has incorporated its migrants with more emphasis on reli-

---

21 For an historical and modern day perspective of the influence of the Pillar system in Dutch society, see Gowricharn & Mungra (1996). The politics of integration in the Netherlands. In Shadid & van Koningsveld (eds.) (1996).
22 'On 11 June 2004 the government [of the R.O.I] asked the electorate to vote in a referendum to amend Article 9 of the Constitution to remove birth-right citizenship from children born in Ireland who do not have at least one parent who is an Irish citizen or who is entitled to Irish Citizenship [...] 79.8 percent of the electorate voted in favour of the government's proposal' (Lentin 2007, p. 610).
23 For a concise table of naturalisation and franchise rights across Europe refer to note 19.

gious recognition by funding religious schools and educational programs and prohibiting religious discrimination through the Equal Status Act 2000.[24]

In spite of a relatively open and liberal civic pluralism, the ROI, according to the Migration Integration Policy Index (MIPEX, 2010), has the least secure long-term residence policy for third country nationals (who do not wish to take up Irish citizenship) in Europe, due to the fact that 'security to live in Ireland for the long-term is discretionary and entirely based on their security of employment'. The same source reports that class inequality also permeates the Irish long-term residence policy as regular workers have to work in Ireland for five years to get a renewable work permit (stamp 4) and eight years to get an indefinite work permit (stamp 6) whilst strategically important occupations (with incomes above €60,000) can be fast-tracked by the Green Card system (MIPEX, 2010).

In terms of franchise rights for third country nationals, the Irish state was one of the first European countries to institutionalise local voting rights based on residency (*ius domicili*) rather than on citizenship. The electoral act of 1963 and the subsequent amendment of 1972 gave the local electoral franchise to third country nationals over 18 years of age and ordinarily resident in a particular constituency (Whelan, 2000, p. 8). In common with nearly all other European states (except the United Kingdom), the national electoral franchise is still not conferred onto third country nationals within the Irish state.[25]

In terms of the Muslim communities' social and political space, the ROI's naturalisation and local election franchise policies are liberal and inclusive compared to most other European states. However, the Muslim community in Ireland has now become electorally stratified: there are Muslims who are citizens[26] and may vote in all Irish elections and referenda (local, national and European); there

---

24 The Equality Status Acts (2000-2004) and the Equality Act 2004 legislate for religious discrimination in goods, services, accommodation, education and employment in the R.O.I. Available from http://www.irishstatutebook.ie/2004/en/act/pub/0024/index.html. Such recognition of religious discrimination may have its roots in the Irish colonial experience of successive British Penal Laws, which (within the 17th and 18th Centuries) reduced Catholic rights and subsequently significantly reduced Catholic land-holdings on the island. See 'Muslim MP calls for religious equality Law'. *The Independent [U.K]*, 16th September 2008. Available at http://www.independent.co.uk/news/uk/politics/muslim-mp-calls-for-religious-equality-law-931982.html. On the 1st October 2010, the Equality Act will come into force in the U.K. An element of this act is recognition of religious discrimination in line with previous European directives.

25 For a concise table of naturalisation and franchise rights across Europe refer to note 19.

26 There are approximately 9, 761 Irish citizens belonging to the Islamic faith. This number comprises individuals who have decided to naturalise, Irish citizens who have converted to the Islamic faith and Irish-born Muslim children. See Central Statistics Office (C.S.O, 2010). *Census 2006 – 'Volume 13 – Religion'*. Available from www.cso.ie.

are Muslims who are E.U. citizens[27] and may vote in local and European elections; and third country nationals of the Islamic faith who as residents of a constituency may vote in local elections for that area only. In an influential study on democracy, citizenship and the nation state, Thomas Hammer (1990) viewed and categorised resident third country nationals who enjoyed a secure and peaceful life within a host country as a new form of status, which he termed 'denizenship'.

Such civic stratification[28] of the Muslim community into citizens and denizens may inhibit the ability of the community to participate politically in a 'conventional' way (i.e. via electoral voting and representation). Alternatively, to act collectively in its interests, the Muslim community may rely more on 'unconventional' means of political participation (i.e. via trade unions, lobbying, community committees and Muslim organisations). Interestingly, citizenship and denizenship stratification within the Irish community may produce significant variations in political integration, which may lead to higher or lower voting levels in local elections. Research by Fennema and Tille (2001) in the Netherlands has shown that the Turkish denizen community participates strongly in local elections in contrast to other migrant communities such as the Surinamese and Antilleans, who have gained Dutch citizenship via colonial affiliation (p. 39).

Current evidence shows a lack of conventional political representation by Muslims at the national and local electoral levels in Ireland. A brief overview of Muslims running in Irish elections shows that only one Muslim has ever been elected to the national parliament – Indian-born Dr. Bhamjee Moosajee, a Labour backbench parliamentarian (Irish: *Teachta Dala, TD*) for County Clare after the 1992 general election.[29] In the 2009 local elections[30], only four Muslim individuals[31] could be identified as having competed for a council seat within their respective

---

27 There are approximately 2,544 European citizens of Islamic faith in the R.O.I, of which 620 are U.K citizens who may vote in the Irish national elections. Approximations from Central Statistics Office (C.S.O, 2010). *Census 2006 – Combined 'Nationality' dataset and 'Volume 13 – Religion'*. Available from www.cso.ie.
28 A term developed by Lockwood (1996).
29 Dr. Bhamjee Moosajee declined to run again in the 1997 General Election but has continued to lobby on behalf of the Muslim community in County Clare. See 'Council to Provide 20 Muslim Graves. *The Irish Times*, 12th December 2007. Available from www.irishtimes.com/search/index.html.
30 The June 2009 Local Elections incorporated 258 separate local elections to elect 1,627 local public representatives (Weeks and Quinlivan 2009, p. 6).
31 Shaheen Ahmed (F.F.) – Lucan 448 – 1st preference votes – Total vote 15,425 – Not Elected.
M. Ahmed (Ind.) – Waterford East – 130 1st preference votes – Total vote 10,094 – Not Elected.
Rashid Butt (Ind.) – Mullingar West – 185 1st preference votes – Total vote 13,526 – Not Elected.
Zahid Hussein (Ind.) – Castleknock – 136 1st preference votes – Total vote 29,622 – Not Elected.
Local election 2009 results available from http://electionsireland.org/results/local/2009local.cfm.

local areas.[32] Surprisingly, although there is an open franchise in local elections, there tends to be an absence of participation at the candidate level within the Muslim community. Weeks and Quinlivan (2009) explained such passivity by the fact that local elections, over the years within the ROI and in contrast to common European practice, have been weakened by a limited authority range for local councils, budgetary dependence on the national government, a restrictive career path to the national political arena for local councillors[33] and a duel mandate[34] tactic practiced by elected TDs to control the political space within local politics. The prohibition of dual mandate in 2003 may provide the further space for denizens to participate in local elections.[35]

It has been argued that denizens should voluntarily naturalize to the recipient country citizenship in order to gain full political and electoral rights. However, in many circumstances, this is not possible due to family links, economic investment concerns or the policy advocated and followed by the sending state in terms of renunciation of citizenship. As Gianluca Parolin's (2009) five-year study into Arab citizenship acknowledges:

> 'If the freedom to change nationality prevails, foreign naturalization automatically entails loss of nationality, whereas if perpetual allegiance proves stronger, loss of nationality for foreign naturalization is subject to state consent' (pp. 108 & 128)[36]

---

32 Further detailed quantitative and qualitative research is needed to discover individual Muslim voting patterns and party preferences within the R.O.I.
33 Many councillors hope to gain a party nomination to run in the national elections. However, a limited number of nominations are available, which may cause disappointment to many local councillors. Between 2006 and 2008, eleven councillors resigned from the fifty-two seat Dublin City Council. See Weeks and Quinlivan (2009, p. 169).
34 Duel Mandate refers to parliamentarians (TDs) holding a national seat alongside a seat on their local council. In 2002, of the 226 elected TDs, 138 were members of their local councils. This practice was prohibited by the 2003 Local Government Act (No. 2). See Weeks and Quinlivan. (2009, pp. 39-40).
35 However, multiple academic reports have shown that Irish political parties have been very slow to implement policies that incorporate immigrant party members and select immigrant electoral candidates. See Fanning, B., Mutawarasibo, F. & Chadmayo, N. (2004); Fanning, Shaw, O'Connell, & Williams. (2007); Fanning, O' Boyle. & Shaw. (2009). All three reports are available from http://www.ucd.ie/mcri/publications.html.
36 Parolin (2009, p.108) also clarifies that 'the punitive deprivation of nationality for having acquired foreign nationality without state permission is the main orientation of Gulf legislation'.

The Irish Educational System and the Muslim Community[37]

From the 1930s to the 1950s, the Catholic Church acquired a leading role within Irish society to the point where the Irish Constitution[38] publically and lawfully acknowledged that position. Although not recognised as the official state religion, this strong relationship between church and state may be viewed as a necessary step in order to establish and formulate an Irish identity distinct to the British identity that had preceded Irish independence. The foundation and perpetuation of this nascent Irish identity was forged by the Catholic Church's domination of the educational system. In 1972, a constitutional amendment was passed which recognised and respected religious practice but ensured the non-endowment of a particular religion. However, the Catholic Church continued to exert traditional conservative power within Irish society at large culminating in fierce debates between various elements of society in relation to issues of divorce, abortion[39] and homosexuality. Notably, although the Irish constitution declared the separation between the various religious establishments and the state, the Catholic Church has continued to dominate the administration of education in Ireland with government support. The position of the Church in this regard has weakened in recent years. Even the Archbishop of Dublin, Dr. Diarmuid Martin, publically acknowledged to the Irish Primary Principals Network (Dublin Network) that the Catholic monopoly of the Irish education system is an 'historical hangover' and that 'a system in which 92 percent of all primary schools [are] managed by the Catholic Church in a country where the Catholic population is 87 percent is certainly not tenable.'[40]

The Irish Constitution's public recognition of religion and its amended statement not to endow any one particular religion has been positively acknowledged by the Irish-Muslim community. Furthermore, the ROI's legacy of denominational and confessional education[41] has also transferred educational and religious space to the Muslim Community. Such educational religious space is guaranteed by the Irish Constitution which acknowledges in Article 42.1 that 'the primary and natural educator of the child is the family and guarantees to respect the inalienable right

---

37 The primary reference to this section unless otherwise stated is Sakaranaho (2006).
38 An online version of the Irish Constitution is available from http://www.taoiseach.ie/eng/Youth_Zone/About_the_Constitution,_Flag,_Anthem_Harp/Constitution_of_IrelandNov2004.pdf.
39 See 'Muslims favour retaining abortion clause in the Constitution'. *The Irish Times*, 6th July 2000. Available from www.irishtimes.com/search/index.html.
40 See 'A New System of School Patronage' and 'Labour Calls on Minister to Review Church Role'. *The Irish Times*, 18th June 2009. Available from www.irishtimes.com/search/index.html.
41 'Confessional' refers to the fostering of commitment to a faith by religious education. As opposed to 'Non-Confessional' which refers to distributing information about varying religions and their practices.

and duty of parents to provide, according to their means, for the religious and moral, intellectual, physical and social education of their children'.[42]

Similar to European citizenship policy, the practice of allowing Muslim communities religious educational freedom varies depending on particular member state laws and policies. As Brigitte Merechal (2003) has stated in relation to this pan-European issue:

> 'Only about half of the European countries have officially recognised and state-supported Islamic schools. As a rule, those schools do not exist in countries with small Muslim populations of which Finland is an example' (pp. 50-51).

If Finland is the example, Ireland is certainly the exception by the fact that the small Muslim population within the Irish state has utilised the use of two Muslim schools for over a twenty year period. The decade of the 1990s heralded the continuing decline of the Catholic Church and an increase in the multicultural nature of the Irish nation as immigration levels increased. As has already been stated above, the increase in the Muslim population created the need for better facilities and for the creation of Islamic education with state support. In 1990, the first Muslim educational facilities in Ireland were established and administered by the IFI By 1993, with the construction of the ICCI near completion; the school was transferred to the more spacious facilities attached to the more modern mosque. This new complex not only contained a library, a centre for women, a restaurant, gym and an accommodation block but also three different Muslim schools: (1) the Muslim National School (Scoil Naisiunta Maslamach), which is administered by the IFI; (2) the Nur-Al-Huda Quranic School, which specialises in the memorisation of the Koran; and (3) a Libyan School, which follows the prescribed Libyan syllabus that is accepted throughout the Middle East. At the national school opening in 1993, the President of Ireland Mary Robinson spoke of the fact that it was 'only natural that members of the Muslim community would feel the need for an education which would reflect the values of the Islamic faith' (IFI, 1993). The Muslim National School follows the standard Irish school curriculum but allows for the school itself to administer religious instruction in the Islamic faith. The school caters to around 300 students of Sunni and Shia orientation. In 2001, a second state funded Muslim national school opened on the north side of Dublin. This school caters to approximately 100 students of Sunni orientation. Notably, in recent years, the north Dublin Muslim National School has received criticism from the Department of Education and the media in relation to high staff turnover levels, financial and enrolment irregularities and time-allocation to curricu-

---

42 Refer to note 37.

lum subjects.[43] As administrators of the school since 2007, the IFI has sought to quickly remedy the above concerns by ensuring all outlying bills are paid to the Department of Education; by introducing a standard child protection policy and training; by introducing curricular plans for subjects such as maths, music and Irish; and regulating the time-allotted to curricular subjects to five hours and ten minutes per day [excluding religious education] (IFI, 2009).

In addition, as in other European countries, the debate related to the wearing of the hijab has begun to surface in the ROI but in a contradictory manner to the discussion and policy in secular France[44]. The subject arose when the Irish Times newspaper printed a correspondence between the Department of Education and the principal of a school which concerned a lack of national policy on the wearing of the hijab within Irish schools.[45] As media attention increased, the government issued a response in which the government categorically stated that 'the issue of a school uniform is one for school authorities to design a policy on, following local consultations with the various members of the local community' (Integration Unit of the Office of the Minister of Integration, 2009). In particular, the Minister for Integration, Conor Lenihan, referenced the Education Act (1998) which clarified the management role for school authorities as one of 'respect for the diversity of values, beliefs, traditions, languages and ways of life in society'. In a submission letter to the Minister for Integration, the IFI strongly criticised the media for its sensationalist reporting and emphasised the unique space available in Ireland under its civic laws:

> the debate on the issue (of the hijab) has been typified by misunderstanding, myth and sensationalism. Opinions on Islam and its practice have been expressed by those unqualified to do so. Media pundits have expressed views on the wearing of the hijab without consulting any mainstream Islamic authority…all citizens no matter their ethnicity or religion should be entitled to the same expression of their beliefs. We have seen the road taken by some of our Eu-

---

43 See 'Department Delivers Scathing Report on Dublin Muslim School'. *The Irish Times*, 18th June 2009; 'Islamic Foundation Defends Running of School after Department's Criticism'. *The Irish Times*, 23rd June 2009. Available from www.irishtimes.com/search/index.html.

44 *L'affaire du Foulard (the scarf affair)* began in October 1989, when the headmaster of the College Gabriel Havez of Creil forbade three female Muslim students from attending class with their heads covered. On the advice of M. Daniel Youssouf Leclerq, a leading Muslim in France, the three girls defied the ban and thereby challenged the boundaries between public and private in the French state. The Conseil d'état or French Supreme Court attempted to balance the principles of *läicité* with religious freedom but ended with an unclear judgement that transferred the responsibility to the sole judgement of the school authorities. On 10 February 2004, the French National Assembly banned the wearing of all religious symbols from public schools. For a more detailed analysis see Benhabib (2004, pp. 184-194).

45 See 'Ministers agree common approach to wearing of Hijab'. *The Irish Times*, 3rd September 2008. Available from www.irishtimes.com/search/index.html.

ropean neighbours where all religious symbols have been removed from schools and rich tapestry of difference lost (IFI, 2008).[46]

The Political Exclusion of the Transnational 'Other'

As has been shown above, the Irish social and political opportunity structure in Ireland creates and presents incentives and disincentives to the domiciled Muslim community. Incentives identified above relate to a political system whose origins and ethos are primarily based on an independence proclamation which aimed to establish universal civil rights and appease a religious minority; the related absence of a RR party; a shared colonial and migratory past; a toleration of dual citizenship; and the religious influence which predominated Irish society and educational institutions since the formation of the state. Importantly, the Irish state has a civic pluralist form of citizenship and incorporation that is reflected in the policy of *ius soli* and respect for cultural and religious difference. In terms of disadvantages, societal racism and the political stratification of the Muslim community into citizens and denizens and the restrictive implications for long term residence, predominate.[47] It must also be recognised that civic stratification of the Muslim community contains a geographic-economic element. Notably, the institutional completeness of the Muslim community is strong primarily in the Dublin region and very much weaker outside of the metropolitan area. For example, the capital city contains three major mosques and affiliated organisations; the only Muslim educational facilities; and the economic resources of the Muslim community as well as close access to pre-existing social and political structures, which have historically resided within the capital. Consequently, the Muslim communities outside Dublin lack institutional completeness and access to advantageous social and political opportunity structures including mosque and social facilities (such as those within the ICCI), denominational education and economic indepen-

---

46 See also 'Imam warns of Irish media hostility'. *The Irish Times*, 6th February 2006. Available from www.irishtimes.com/search/index.html.
47 For a discussion about the duality of legitimacy claims by 'nationals' and 'non-nationals' in terms of the 2004 Irish Citizenship Referendum – see Fanning and Mutwarasibo (2007). Furthermore, Fanning (2004) has given a good account of state-endorsed civic stratification by stating that 'immigrant workers, immigrants with Irish-born children, people with refugee status and asylum seekers are each deemed by the state to have different levels of rights and entitlements. In all cases, these are less than the entitlements of citizens. Distinctions between the entitlements of a number of such non-citizen groups are the result of state decisions that categorise and stratify people for administrative and political purposes' (p. 67).

dence. Subsequently, many of the regional Muslim communities are dependent and reliant upon the organisations based in Dublin, such as the IFI and ICCI.[48]

However overall, in terms of the social and political structure, it can be argued that the institutionalised system of migrants' political incorporation remains an arena of exclusion, which is controlled and maintained by the nation state. Thus, from a critical cosmopolitan perspective, it is possible to conclude that the power dynamic between nation states and migrants is one-sided. In other words, it is the nation state system that has designed the process by which migrants select a citizen or denizen political identity. Fundamentally, civic stratification of the migrant political arena is a power mechanism actively employed by nation states in order to maintain power and control via selective exclusion of resident peoples from the national political community. By excluding distinct and differentiated people from substantial political participation, the nation state is actively restricting the domestic political identity of its denizen population, and consequently, refocusing the innate political dimension of the denizen towards unconventional political participation domestically and political involvement in a transnational sense. This becomes even more pronounced in the ROI, since local authorities have been disenfranchised from political and financial power. This is morally reprehensible from a cosmopolitan human rights perspective. This point is backed by an Intergovernmental Committee for Migration [ICM] conference:

'The migrant's integration – apart from economic, social and cultural aspects – involves the question of political participation, since the migrant has a political dimension, as does any human being; his status in the receiving country cannot be divorced from this fundamental dimension' (ICM Conference, 1976, p. 78).

Within the next section, we will extrapolate how the moral sensitivity of critical cosmopolitan theory, with a particular attention on Andrew Linklater's transformative framework, can provide a remedy to continued and persistent civic stratification of the Muslim population into citizens and denizens and realign the performance of the Irish political community onto a more equitable and moral existence. We will also highlight our belief that the restriction of denizens from the full political community in the ROI is refocusing political action into non-conventional forms of political participation that has a national and transnational remit.

---

48 See 'Why Cork's Muslim Community wants a Mosque'. *The Irish Times*, 24th February 1998. Available from www.irishtimes.com/search/index.html.

Revisiting Linklater's Transformation of the Political Community

Critical Theory is essentially a social critique that has the specific goal of identifying exclusionary practices within human society and then attempting to emancipate individuals from those exclusionary practices. It aims to subvert neorealist immutability claims (Linklater, 2007).[49] The strength of critical theory lies in its ability to 'debunk conventional assumptions about the natural qualities of social structures or human behaviour and to identify countervailing and progressive tendencies within existing societies' (Linklater, 1998, p. 44).

Andrew Linklater's critical international theories are important in that they attempt to emancipate individuals within the domestic environment in order to affect change at the international level. Within *The Transformation of the Political Community,* Linklater theorises the continuing decline of the nation state's monopoly over the political community and determines that the international anarchic community can be pacified by morally broadening the scope of the political community to include previously excluded actors such as aliens and non-citizens who are domiciled within the nation state. He highlighted the aim of his book by stating that the 'central purpose is to reaffirm the cosmopolitan critique of the sovereign state-system and to defend the widening of the moral boundaries of political communities' (Linklater, p. 2). His theory, in line with Kant and Marx, is morally constituted, cosmopolitan, humanistic and against exclusion (Linklater, 1990). It is also postmodern in that it rejects binary classifications, respects the fragmented composition of modern societies and aims to transcend the state structure. Linklater (1998) foresees the triple transformation of the political community. By this, he means a frame of mind and discursive practice that secures 'greater respect for cultural differences, stronger commitments to the reduction of material inequalities and significant advances in universality [to] resist pressures to contract the boundaries of community' (p. 3).[50] A central theoretical ambition is to disconnect the link between sovereignty, territoriality, nationality and citizenship, which has been propagated by the nation state and moulded into a stereotype of political community.

Notably, for Linklater, the political community has been totalised by the sovereign powers over time. The nation state has monopolised the right to control the

---

49 The immutability thesis claims that 'social structures or forms of human action are natural and unchangeable rather than contingent and renegotiable'. Linklater (2007, pp. 47-48).

50 In contra to the cosmopolitan perspective, communitarians such as Michael Walzer believe that citizens are inextricably linked to bounded communities through a shared historical experience and that nation states have 'the right to decide who can become a member and who should be turned away' (Linklater, 2007, pp. 109-112). See Walzer, M. (2002). Spheres of affection. In Nussbaum, M. (ed.), *For love of country?* Boston MA: Beacon Press.

instruments of violence; the right to tax citizens; the ordering of political allegiance; the right to adjudicate disputes between citizens; and the right to represent citizens in the international arena (Linklater, 1998 p. 28). This totalising of the political community has maintained and legitimised the exclusion of outsiders and the overwhelming inclusion and protection of specific groups of insiders. This in itself stunts moral development within the community and perpetuates a moral democratic paradox in which the state on the one hand protects individuals but also excludes and disenfranchises 'other' individuals for reasons which cannot be morally accepted in the modern global era.

Within the totalised Irish community, it has been demonstrated that Muslim third country nationals are excluded from the full political community (as long as they remain within the realm of denizenship). David Held (1995) created the term *nautonomy* to refer to the 'asymmetrical production and distribution of life-chances which limit and erode the possibilities of political action' (p. 171). Furthermore, social and political stratification is referenced as perpetuating exclusionary practices that form the 'capability of groups to exclude 'outsiders' and to control resources denied to others' (Held, pp.171 & 185). To transcend these stratifying and exclusionary practices, Held determines that individuals can acquire autonomy via cosmopolitan democratic law, which is 'a democratic public entrenched within and across borders' (p. 227).[51]

The totalising nation state reached its zenith with the Nazi and Soviet regimes, which both promoted a 'dominant conception of national identity' (Linklater, 1998, p. 7),[52] but has been in steady decline as mass globalised immigration and movement have fragmented the domestic communities of nation states. Such globalisation and fragmentation 'erode traditional conceptions of community and reduce the moral significance of national boundaries' (Linklater, p. 5). In terms of the citizen and denizen dichotomy, the nation state has lost its ethical foundation for preserving this stratification within the bounded political community. Moral responsibility has shifted beyond the enclosed *polis* to those outside and to those inside but excluded. In the modern global era,

---

51 In opposition to Held, Kymlicka (1999, pp. 112-125) is pessimistic about including individuals within transnational institutions and about constructing effective democratic and collective will above the nation state. Moreover, although enthusiastic about cosmopolitan possibilities, Wendt (1999, pp. 137-132) foresees a cosmopolitan system made up of states rather than individuals. These states will then be able to disseminate a transnational identity and respect to their citizens.

52 Cosmopolitans' insist that new global economic, technological and ecological realms as well as the strengthening of international human rights and non-governmental organisations (INGO's) have undermined national boundaries and have therefore weakened the sovereignty of nation states. (Cf. Held, 1995; Archibuggi, 2008; Linklater, 1990, 1998, 2007; Soysal, 1994; Jacobson, 1997; Benhabib, 2004).

'one of the constitutive ethical principles of the sovereign state has lost its status as a self evident truth: this is the belief that the welfare of co-nationals takes precedence over the interests of aliens' (Linklater, 2007, p. 80).

This thereby makes it no longer a utopian ideal 'to imagine new forms of political community and new conceptions of citizenship which bind sub-state, state and transnational society' (Linklater, 1998, p. 8). Exclusionary practices can be eroded by moral empathy and the formation of a dialogic community that places discourse at the top of its agenda.

In the modern era, global networks of communication have made it much harder for nation states to control and regulate the political composition of their citizens and long-term residents, thereby, leading to a weakening of the totalising characteristic of the nation state structure. Certainly, as Yasemin Soysal (1994) writes: 'although nation-states still protect their membership by controlling the inflow of foreigners, an expanding range of rights and privileges is being granted to [...] migrants, blurring the line between citizen and non-citizen' (p. 130). Soysal argues against T.H Marshall's (1964) 'rights' sequence'[53] by suggesting that the individual libertarian nature of civil and social rights delineates noticeably from political rights that still convey a collective and 'symbolic meaning in terms of national sovereignty' (p. 131). Interestingly, this point may suggest the variation and discrepancy between social and political rights for immigrants within the Irish nation (and other European states). However, Soysal believes that 'the logic of personhood supersedes the logic of national citizenship' (p. 164) and that political rights can be transformed within the state into new modalities of postnational citizenship, which allow Muslim denizens within the Irish state to be recognized as political entities with national and transnational rights.[54]

Linklater (1998) emphasises that one 'should not underrate the power of the nation-state and its enduring capacity to rally support' (p. 33). Recognising the changing political environment, many European countries have allowed the once excluded – aliens and third country nationals – to vote in local elections. Although recent recruitment drives for electoral registering have been successful,[55] it must be remembered that Irish local politics is significantly limited in relation to its European counterparts. Moreover, the important arena of the national electoral vote is still reserved for the full members of the political community and

---

53 Marshall's (1964) model places rights acquisition in the sequence: civil, political and then social.
54 Soysal's postnational citizenship perspective is heavily criticised by the content analysis work of Koopmans and Statham who object to the fact that migrant claims making is significantly postnational. In fact, they believe that the state remains the main focus of migrant claims-making. (Koopmans and Statham 1999, 2000, 2001).
55 See 'Number of migrants voting in local elections rises 44%'. *The Irish Times*, 16th June 2010. Available from www.irishtimes.com/search/index.html.

persistently blocked by extremely long citizenship application procedures that can take up to eight years (four to five years for the right to apply and then three years for the application to be processed). In the words of Issah Huseini of the New Communities Partnership, which aims to encourage immigrant registration and voting in the ROI, these barriers 'reinforce the perception that immigrants are outsiders notwithstanding the number of years they've lived in the country'.[56] Fundamentally, nation states have come to realise the need to entice the excluded denizen into the full political community (albeit within a timeframe regulated by the state authorities) by ensuring that the existing social and political opportunity structures create a demand for full citizenship. This strategy allows the nation state to maintain control of the political community and transfer moral responsibility from the state to the individual choice of the excluded person.

From a critical theory perspective, the exclusion of domiciled individuals from the national vote creates the entity of an 'other' and also fosters divisions within subaltern communities by demarcating sections within these communities as full citizens or non-citizens. Certainly, this exclusion does not rest easy with the modern cosmopolitan ethic of equality. Linklater (1998) disagrees with civic stratification via citizenship control. He suggests that 'no individuals should be excluded by virtue of their class, nationality, ethnicity, sexual identity, gender or race from participating in decisions which impinge upon their welfare and interests' (p. 103).

Overall, there are positive and negative incentives related to the move from being a denizen with cosmopolitan transnational associations to a full member of the Irish political community. In terms of Linklater's post-Westphalian theory, it could be said that the Irish nation-state, in order to preserve its own control and power over the political community, is actively promoting the transition from denizenship to citizenship. Therefore, instead of fulfilling its own moral obligations to humanity, the Irish nation state has moved the responsibility for exclusion to the excluded person. In other words, the denizen is given a choice between being a cosmopolitan transnational entity with limited rights and recognition or a full member of the Irish political community, who has full political rights and protection by default.[57] Consequently, the Irish nation state is effectively absolved from any

---

56 Refer to note 55.
57 It must be recognised that Muslims domiciled within the R.O.I may also be actively choosing to remain within the realm of denizenship. Roy (2004) has touched on this point by suggesting that Muslim groups (particularly neo-fundamentalist groups) are actively promoting a de-territorialised existence that bypasses ethnic and national cleavages in order to develop a 'pure' unmediated form of Islam – an Islam that cannot be abused by the self-interest of nation states and can be identified as a 'cosmopolitan' Ummah. Also, Baubock (1994) has stated that low naturalisation rates may be reflective of the fact that denizens enjoy many civil and social rights that full citizens enjoy (except for political rights).

humanitarian and moral responsibility. Although aspects of state power are in decline, the Irish nation state remains in control of the political community and actively excludes denizens (i.e. individuals who have not declared their allegiance to the Irish state) from the full electoral process. Furthermore, if dual citizenship is unattainable, the policies of other nation states (i.e. an immigrant's country of origin) may also inhibit the ability of a denizen from becoming part of the full political community within the receiving country.

The question must be asked as to what effect does the restriction from the full political community have on denizens and their political participation? We would suggest that the exclusion of denizens from the full political community in the ROI refocuses political participation away from conventional political action such as voting and running for electoral office and into modes of unconventional participation that involve lobbying, street protestation and media discourse. Non-conventional forms of political action are generally collective and have national and transnational[58] focus. Marco Martinello (2006) has emphasised that 'relevant political participation cannot be reduced to electoral participation. Other forms such as trade union politics, association and community organisation have to be taken into account as well' (p. 86). Martinello and Lafleur (2008), developing on Østergaard-Nielsen's (2003) transnational activity typology of homeland, immigrant and translocal politics, prefer not to design a category that risks giving 'the impression that spaces of political action are clearly separated from one another' (pp.652-653) and instead form a broad definition of immigrant political transnationalism. This definition states that:

> 'Immigrant political transnationalism covers any political activity undertaken by migrants who reside mainly outside their homeland and that is aimed at gaining political power or influence at the individual or collective level in the country of residence or in the state to which they consider they belong. Such power or influence may be achieved by interacting with all kinds of institutions (local, subnational, national or international) in the country of residence and/or the home country, by supporting movements that are politically active in the country of origin or by intervening directly in the country of origin's politics' (Martinello and Lafleur, pp. 652-653).

---

58 Transnationalism has been defined a process by which 'immigrants forge and sustain multi-stranded social relations that link together their societies of origin and settlement [...] many immigrants today build social fields that cross geographic, cultural, and political borders'. See Basch, Glick Schiller and Blanc-Szanton (1994, p. 7). Martinello and Lafleur believe the above classical definition 'contains three major elements in the apprehension of immigrant transnationalism. First, it implies that the links between the individual and the nation-state are not exclusive but multiple [...] Second, the space within which the migrants work, conduct their social, political and religious lives or even raise a family cannot be clearly divided between the home and receiving country [...] Third, this definition implies that transnationalism potentially concerns every aspect of a migrants' life. Yet, the intensity of transnational political activity may vary substantially from one individual to another' (Martinello & Lafleur, 2008, pp. 648-649).

Notably, the Irish Times newspaper gives some indication of nonconventional political participation with national and transnational focus. For example, demonstrations and lobbying by Muslim groups in the ROI in relation to proposed banning of the veil in France; street protests by Islamic students against the Iraq occupation and use of Shannon airport as a U.S military stopover; further street protests against the cartoon depiction of Muhammad within various European newspapers (including the reproduction of the cartoon within the Irish tabloid – *The Star*); the lobbying of Irish banks to facilitate Islamic banking for the Irish Muslim community; and further lobbying of the Irish government and the European Union to intervene in the Israeli-Palestinian and Israeli-Lebanese conflicts.[59] Unfortunately, this point cannot be expanded further because newspaper coverage gives a limited view of unconventional national and transnational activity.[60]

It can be said that the Irish nation state is not morally righteous in its exclusion of denizens from the national vote and from automatic citizenship.[61] In Linklater's (1998) own words, 'the boundaries of the political community have not coincided with the boundaries of the moral community' (p. 155). By this he is arguing that although governments are under no responsibility to admit persons hostile to the state or without regard to economic and social circumstances, overall, there is no moral reasoning that can explain the exclusion of persons from the

---

59 See 'Thousands protest at ban on headscarves' 19th January 2004; 'An Irishman's Diary' 25th March 2005; 'Muslims in Dublin cartoon protest march' 11th February 2006; 'Muslim groups here urge stronger Irish stance' 5th August 2006; 'New body launched to represent Muslims in Ireland' 19th September 2006; 'Call of Islamic Mortgage Scheme' 25th June 2007; 'Islamic Banking: Now demanded in the Republic' 13 August 2007; 'Group to lobby for right to wear hijab' 2nd September 2008; 'Muslims auction their cars to help raise funds for Gaza' 10th January 2009; 'Scuffles break out at rival protests' 12th January 2009. All available from *The Irish Times*: www.irishtimes.com/search/index.html. See also *The Friday Times*. (April 2003-April 2005). Available from the National Library of Ireland (NLI) (Holding Number: IK 450). www.nli.ie/en/catalogues-and-databases-printed-newspapers.aspx. Notably, *The Friday Times* is the first and only newspaper to be produced specifically for the Muslim community in Ireland. However, its viewpoints were not holistically representative of the Muslim community in the ROI.

60 We hope to investigate the link between exclusion from the full political community and non-conventional national-transnational political action in the future by conducting a quantitative survey of a random sample of the Muslim population domiciled in the Dublin metropolitan area.

61 Linklater's cosmopolitan theory does seem to have a more anti-state and open position to the acquisition of citizenship than Benhabib (2004) who declares that: 'I have pleaded for moral universalism and cosmopolitan federalism. I have not advocated open but rather porous borders [...and] have accepted the right of democracies to regulate the transition from first admission to full membership' (p. 221). Essentially, Benhabib calls for more adherence to human rights within the territorial boundaries of the state whilst Linklater asks for a moral discourse that will lead to a transcendence of the Westphalian state system.

political community simply due to their belonging or birth within another state (Linklater, pp. 57 & 80).

It can therefore be stated that the Irish nation's civic stratification of the Muslim community into denizens and citizens is morally indefensible. Ideally, the Irish nation should be prepared to involve everyone within its borders in the full political community. In other words, citizenship and the right to vote in all elections should be open to all and excluded to nobody. This suggests that the Irish nation should actively take steps to enlarge the boundaries of the moral and political community so that all affected parties – citizens and denizens – can work together as co-legislators (Linklater, 1998, p. 84).

Citizenship, throughout history, 'has possessed its own forward momentum' (Linklater, 1998, p. 185) and ability to expand the boundaries of political community. In addition, the idea of citizenship has been continuously re-articulated to give a political vote and voice to groups that had been at one time or another excluded from the circle of representation. Interestingly, the ROI has played an innovative lead role in extending citizenship rights in Europe. Ireland was one of the first countries to give denizens the local vote based on residence (*ius domicili*) instead of citizenship yet, in common with the majority of other European nations; it has stopped short of its moral commitment to open the boundaries to the national vote and automatic citizenship. Linklater (1998) describes restriction to citizenship as 'a key weapon in the exercise of monopolising social privileges and opportunities' (p. 189).[62] It may be suggested therefore that the Republic of Ireland, whilst allowing for some allowances to the post-modern era, is unwilling to give up its monopoly to citizenship and control of the full political community. In fact, it is up to the denizen to make a political decision as to which camp to deposit his/her allegiance, whilst the nation state denies its own moral obligations to humanity. Therefore, the nation state maintains and receives political power by being the gate-keeper of rights. From a critical perspective, modern Ireland needs to come to terms with the tensions that exist within modern citizenship and its impact on subaltern communities domiciled within its borders. As Linklater has suggested:

> 'the modern idea of citizenship is laden with tensions and instabilities. On the one hand, citizenship embodies the right to freedom and equality which is the property of the whole of humanity; on the other hand, citizenship is invested in separate political communities which can happily purchase their own autonomy by limiting the freedom of others' (1998, p. 191).

Realistically, how can so many diverging viewpoints be accommodated within a community with an open policy on the acquisition of citizenship? This is where

---

62 In America, academic literature on noncitizen voting is small but growing. See Raskin (1993) and Hayduk (2004). Critics of noncitizen voting see the process as likely to devalue the worth of citizenship. See Schuck (1998).

Linklater's theory freely mixes with the Habermasian idea of discourse ethics (Habermas 1989, p.82ff). This idea suggests that a heterogeneous political community that is fully open to universal discourse can resolve societal issues and formulate equitable solutions. The Habermasian notion of true dialogue refers to a mutual reciprocal exchange whereby no person, group or moral position can be excluded from the dialogue in advance. In other words, the dialogue is an open and mutual process. Habermas (1990) succinctly described true dialogue as

> "not a trial of strength between adversaries hell-bent on intellectual conquest, but an encounter in which human beings accept that there is no a priori certainty about who will learn from whom, and engage in a process of 'reciprocal critique' which is designed to create social arrangements which meet the consent of all" (p. 26).

Logically, a political community that is committed to discourse 'will be deeply concerned about the damaging effects of its actions on outsiders' (Linklater, 1998, p. 91). Participants within this mutual discourse agree to be guided by 'the force of better argument' (Habermas, 1990, pp. 66 & 89) and understand that norms cannot be standardised until they receive the consent of those who stand to be affected by them (Habermas, 1989, p. 82 ff). Fundamentally, discourse ethics disrupts the perpetual norm of territorial sovereignty and of bounded political communities that reinforce exclusion of domiciled and external groups. It does this by problematising 'all social boundaries, including the effects of bounded political communities on the members of other groups' (Linklater, 2007, p. 57). With this in mind, it is possible to conclude from a moral and humanistic perspective that Muslim denizens in the ROI should not be adversely restricted (by process or long periods of time) from the arena of the full political Irish community and the right to participate in important national elections which affect their everyday lives within the state. Therefore, greater representation is not just given to outsiders of the bounded territory: 'one must also envisage communities that recognize the claims of the culturally [and politically] marginal within their boundaries and promote their representation' (Linklater, p. 58).

Furthermore, external political communities who are also affected by domestic realm policies and actions must be given an opportunity to join the discourse (i.e. immigrant sending states). This is confirmed by Seyla Benhabib (2004) who states that since 'discourse theory articulates a universalist moral standpoint, it cannot limit the scope of the moral conversation only to those who reside within the nationally recognised boundaries; it must view moral conversation as potentially extending to all humanity' (p. 14). Benhabib confirms that the transforming of political community exclusion can be reduced through the deployment of *juris-generative* acts, whose praxis is formulated on an iterative democratic process that 'signals a space of interpretation and intervention between intranscendent norms and the will of democratic majorities' (2004, p. 181). Thus, making it possible for the Irish political majority to reassess and reinterpret existing exclusionary norms and in turn transform their political community in a more cosmopolitan direction. This point is confirmed by Benhabib when she states that

> 'Transformations of citizenship, through which rights are extended to individuals by virtue of residency rather than cultural identity, are the clearest forms of such cosmopolitan norms' (2004, p. 177).

The dialogic process of development and the aim to rid the Irish state of systematic and institutional systems of exclusion, will begin the Habermasian process of moral-practical learning, which involves a 'willingness to question all social and political boundaries and all systems of inclusion and exclusion [and to ask ...] whether the boundaries between insiders and outsiders can be justified by principles that are agreeable to all' (Linklater, 2007, p. 51). Producing these characteristics within all nation states can effectively led to the transformation of the political community and the transcending of the Westphalian state system, thereby, creating a international system devoid of perpetual anarchy and characterised by universal discourse and a concern for the other.

Overall, the evidence presented in this paper shows that elements of the Muslim community are excluded from participating within the full political community in Ireland. This immoral exclusion *may* be refocusing denizen political participation into unconventional forms and redirecting political involvement into a more transnational direction. This has come about because the survival of the Irish nation state depends on maintaining its position as the gatekeeper of the political community, which consequently thereby restricts denizens from becoming fully functional political beings. The existence of denizens within nation states is proof that the globalised and fragmented post-modern world has come into being and that such a transformation of the international system is presenting contentious moral dilemmas for the existing Westphalian system. Ultimately, how will post-Westphalian citizenship change in terms of the pre-existing norm? Linklater declares that:

> "Citizens of the post-Westphalian state [...] can come under the jurisdiction of several political authorities; they can have multiple identities and they need not be united by bonds that make them either indifferent, or enemies of, the rest of the human race. The 'Westphalian' state defends national interests against outsiders and frequently takes little account of minority groups within its borders; the post-Westphalian state can remove these moral deficits by striking a new balance between substate loyalties, traditional nation-state attachments and sphere of cosmopolitical identification" (p. 107).

Critical theory proposes a further evolution of citizenship and a continued resistance to the closing of political boundaries. Neo-realists may criticise this constructivist viewpoint as idealist and utopian but the concluding words of Andrew Linklater's seminal book *The Transformation of Political Community* can provide inspiration to challenge neo-realist certainties:

"Maybe visions of a humanity united in domination-free communication will always be utopian. But by unfolding their distinctive moral potentials, modern societies may yet prove capable of creating dialogic arrangements which are unique in the history of world political organisation. Realising the promise of the post-Westphalian era is the essence of the unfinished project of modernity" (Linklater, 1998, p.220).

References

Archibugi, D. (2008). *The Global Commonwealth of Citizens: Toward Cosmopolitan Democracy.* Princeton, N.J: Princeton University Press.

Basch, L., Glick Schiller, N., & Blanc-Szanton, C. (1994). *Nations Unbound: Transnational Projects, Postcolonial Predicaments and Deterritorialised Nation-States.* New York: Gordon & Breach.

Baubock, R. (1994). *Transnational Citizenship: Membership and Rights in International Migration.* London: Sage.

–, (Ed.) (2006) *Migration and Citizenship: Legal Status, Rights and Political Participation [Imiscoe Report].* Amsterdam: Amsterdam University Press.

Benhabib, S. (2004). *The Rights of Others: Aliens, Residents and Citizens.* Cambridge: Cambridge University Press.

Brubaker, R. (1992). *Citizenship and Nationhood in France and Germany.* Cambridge: Harvard University Press.

Central Statistics Office (CSO, 2010). *Census 2006.* Retrieved 10th March, 2010. Available from www.cso.ie.

Education Act 1998. *Section 15(2).* Dublin: Stationery Office. Available from http://www.irishstatutebook.ie/1998/en/act/pub/0051/index.html.

Fanning, B. (2004). Denizens and Citizens. In Peillon, M. & Corcoran, M. (Eds.), *Place and Non-Place: The Reconfiguration of Ireland.* Dublin: Institute of Public Administration.

Fanning, B. and Mutwarasibo, F. (2007). Nationals/Non-Nationals: Immigration, Citizenship and Politics in the Republic of Ireland. *Ethnic and Racial Relations, 30*(3), 439-460

Fanning, B., Mutawarasibo, F. & Chadmayo, N. (2004). *Positive Politics: Participation of Immigrants and Ethnic Minorities in the Electoral Process.* Dublin: Africa Solidarity Centre.

Fanning, B., O' Boyle, N. & Shaw, J. (2009). *New Irish Politics: Political Parties and Immigrants in 2009.* Dublin: Migration and Citizenship Research Initiative [M.C.R.I].

Fanning, B., Shaw, J., O'Connell, J.A., & Williams, M. (2007). *Irish Political Parties: Immigration and Integration in 2007.* Dublin: Migration and Citizenship Research Initiative [M.C.R.I].

Fennema, M. & Tillie, J. (2001). Civic Community, Political Participation and Political Trust of Ethnic Groups, *Connections. 24*(1), 26-41.

Flynn, K. (2006). Understanding Islam in Ireland. *Islam and Christian-Muslim Relations, 17*(2), 223-238.

Garner, S. (2007). Ireland and Immigration: Explaining the Absence of the far Right. *Patterns of Prejudice, 41*(2), 109-130.

Gowricharn, R. & Mungra, B. (1996). The Politics of Integration in the Netherlands. In Shadid, W.A.R. and van Koningsveld, P.S. (Eds.). *Muslims in the Margins: Political Responses to the Presence of Islam in Western Europe.* Kampen: Kok Pharos.

Habermas, J. (1989). *The Theory of Communicative Action, Vol. 2: The Critique of Functionalist Reason.* London: Heinemann.

–, (1990). *Moral Consciousness and Communicative Action.* Cambridge: Polity Press.

Hammer, T. (1990). *Democracy and the Nation State: Aliens, Denizens and Citizens in a World of International Migration.* Aldershot: Ashgate.

Hayduk, R. (2004). Democracy for all: Restoring Immigrant Voting Rights in the US. *New Political Science, 26*(4), 499-523.

Held, D. (1995). *Democracy and the Global Order: From the Modern State to Cosmopolitan Governance.* U.K: Polity Press.

Integration Unit of the Office of the Minister of Integration. (2009). *Report on the Need for a Guidance Note to Schools when Reviewing their Policies on School Uniforms.* Dublin: Stationery Office. Available from http://www.islaminireland.com/documents/uniform_recommendations(2).pdf.

Intergovernmental Committee for Migration (ICM) Conference. (1976). *Third Seminar on Adaptation and Integration of Permanent Immigrants: Conclusions and Recommendations, 14*(1-2), 17-83. Available from Wiley Library Online: doi/10.1111/j.1468-2435.1976.tb00401.x

Islamic Foundation of Ireland (IFI). (1993). *Speech by President of Ireland Mary Robinson [issued April 1993].* Retrieved 6th March 2010. Available from http://www.islaminireland.com/mns.html.

–, (IFI). (2008). *Wearing Islamic Head Cover (hijab) in Irish Schools: A Submission to the Minister for Integration as Part of his Consultation Process on the Issue (Issued 03rd July 2008).* Available from http://www.islaminireland.com/index.html.

–, (IFI). (2009). *North Dublin Muslim School [Statement issued 22nd June 2009].* Retrieved 3rd March 2010. Available from http://www.islaminireland.com/index.html.

Jacobson, D. (1996). *Rights Across Borders: Immigration and the Decline of Citizenship.* London: John Hopkins University Press.

Koopmans, R. and Statham, P. (1999). Challenging the Liberal Nation State? Postnationalism, Multiculturalism, and the Collective Claims Making of Migrants and Ethnic Minorities in Britain and Germany, *American Journal of Sociology*, *105*(3), 652-696.

–, (2000). Migration and Ethnic Relations as a Field of Political Contention: An Opportunity Structure Approach. In Koopmans, R. and Statham, P. (Eds.), *Challenging Immigration and Ethnic Relations Politics: Comparative European Perspectives*. Oxford: Oxford University Press.

–, (2001). 'How National Citizenship Shapes Transnationalism. A Comparative Analysis of Migrant Claims-Making in Germany, Great Britain and the Netherlands'. *Revue Eurohernne des Migrations Internationales*, *17*(2), 63-100.

Kymlicka, W. (1999). Citizenship in an Era of Globalisation: Commentary on Held. In Shapiro, I. & Hacker-Gordon, C. (Eds.), *Democracy's Edges*. U.K: Cambridge University Press.

Lentin, R. (2007). Ireland: Racial State and Crisis Racism. *Ethnic and Racial Studies*, *30*(4), 610-627.

Linklater, A. (1990). *Beyond Realism and Marxism: Critical Theory and International Relations*. U.K: MacMillan Press Ltd.

–, (1998). *The Transformation of Political Community*. Oxford: Polity Press.

–, (Ed.). (2007). *Critical Theory and World Politics: Citizenship, Sovereignty and Humanity*. U.K: Routledge.

Lockwood, D. (1996). Civic Stratification and Class Formation. *British Journal of Sociology*, *47*(3), 531-550.

Marshall. T.H. (1964). *Class, Citizenship and Social Development*. Garden City, N.Y.: Doubleday.

Martinello, M. (2006). Political Participation, Mobilisation and Representation of their Immigrants and their Offspring in Europe. In Baubock, R. (Ed.), *Migration and Citizenship: Legal Status, Rights and Political Participation [Imiscoe report]*. Amsterdam: Amsterdam University Press.

Martinello, M. & Lafleur, J.M. (2008). Towards a Transatlantic Dialogue in the Study of Immigrant Political Transnationalism. *Ethnic and Racial Studies*, *31* (4), 645-663.

Merechal, B. (2003). Modalities of Islamic Instruction. In Marechal, B., Allievi, S., Dassetto, F., Nielsen, J. (Eds.), *Muslim in an Enlarged Europe: Religion and Society*. Leiden, Boston: Brill.

Migration Integration Policy Index (MIPEX). (2010). *Country Profile: Ireland*. Retrieved 30th March, 2010. Available from http://www.integrationindex.eu/topics/2412.html.

Minkenberg, M. (2003). The West European Radical Right as a Collective Actor: Modeling the Impact of Cultural and Structural Variables on Party Formation and Movement Mobilisation. *Comparative European Politics, 1*(2), 149-170.

National Consultative Committee on Racism and Interculturalism (NCRRI). (2005-2008). *Related to Racism and Strategic Responses from the NCCRI* [Six monthly Reports]. Retrieved November 03, 2009. Available from http://www.nccri.ie/incidents-reports.html.

National Consultative Committee on Racism & Interculturalism (NCCRI) and Equality Authority (EA). (2001). *Ireland: Anti-Islamic Reactions in the E.U After the Terrorist Acts Against the USA, 12TH September to 31st December 2001.* Vienna: European Monitoring Centre on Racism and Xenophobia (E.U.M.C).

O'Malley, E. (2008). Why is there no Radical Right Party in Ireland? *West European Politics, 31*(5), 960-977.

Østergaard-Nielsen, E. (2003). *Transnational Politics: Turks and Kurds in Germany.* London: Routledge.

Parolin, G.P. (2009). *Citizenship in the Arab world: Kin, Religion and the Nation-State [Imiscoe Report].* Amsterdam: Amsterdam University Press.

Purdam, K. (1996). Settler Political Participation: Muslim Local Councillors. In Shadid, W.A.R. and van Koningsveld, P.S. (Eds.), *Political Participation and Identities of Muslims in Non-Muslim States.* Kampen: Kok Pharos.

Raskin, J.B. (1993). Legal Aliens, Local Citizens: The Historical Constitutional and Theoretical Meanings of Alien Suffrage. *University of Pennsylvania Law Reviews, 141*(4), 1391-1470.

Roy, O. (2004). *Globalised Islam: The Search for a New Ummah.* London: Hurst & Co.

Rydgen, J. (2004). Explaining the Emergence of the Radical Right-Wing Populist Parties: The Case of Denmark. *West European Politics, 27*(3), 474-502.

Sakaranaho, T. (2006). *Religious Freedom, Multiculturalism, Islam: Crossreading Finland and Ireland [Muslim Minorities Series Volume 6].* Leiden: Brill.

Schuck, P. (1998). *Citizens, Strangers and In-Betweens: Essays on Immigration and Citizenship.* Colorado: Westview Press.

Soysal, Y. (1994). *The Limits of Citizenship: Migrants and Postnational Membership in Europe.* Chicago: University of Chicago.

Walzer, M. (2002). Spheres of Affection. In Nussbaum, M. (ed.), *For Love of Country?* Boston, M.A.: Beacon Press.

Weeks, L. and Quinlivan, A. (2009). *All Politics is Local: A Guide to Local Elections in Ireland.* Cork: Collins Press.

Wendt, A. (1999). A comment on Held's Cosmopolitanism. In Shapiro, I. & Hacker-Gordon, C. (Eds.), *Democracy's Edges.* U.K: Cambridge University Press.

Whelan, N. (2000). *Politics, Elections and Law.* Dublin: Blackhall.

List of Authors

Jakob Egholm Feldt (feldt@ruc.dk)
Ph.D. Associate Professor of Modern History at the Institute for Culture and Identity at Roskilde University, Denmark. Jakob has specialised in Jewish identity making in Israel and the wider Jewish diaspora and also more generally in cultural East-West encounters and identity making in European history from the early 20th Century onwards.

Kirstine Sinclair (sinclair@hist.sdu.dk)
Ph.D. Assistant Professor at the Institute for History and Civilization (Centre for Contemporary Middle East Studies) at the University of Southern Denmark. Kirstine's field of expertise is Muslim minorities in Western Europe and Islamist organisations specifically.

Des Delaney (des.delaney6@mail.dcu.ie)
Ph.D. Candidate in the School of Law and Government, Dublin City University. Des' research focuses on the political attitudes and voting behaviour of Irish Muslims.

Francesco Cavatorta (francesco.cavatorta@dcu.ie)
Ph.D. Senior Lecturer at the School of Law and Government, Dublin City University, Ireland, and Research Fellow at the knowledge Programme West Asia, HIVOS, and the University of Amsterdam. Francesco researches and publishes widely within the field of civil society and democratization in the Arab world, radical Islamic groups in North Africa and international relations of the Middle East and North Africa.

Ehab Galal (ehab@hum.ku.dk)
Ph.D. Assistant Professor in Modern Islam and Middle East Studies at the Department of Cross-Cultural and Regional Studies, University of Copenhagen. Ehab's main research field concerns religious identity construction with regard to use of Arabic satellite media.

Ann-Sophie Hemmingsen (ahe@diis.dk)
Ph.D. Post.doc. at the Danish Institute for International Studies. Ann-Sophies research focuses on modes of identification in relation to jihadism and terrorism.

Birgitte Schepelern Johansen (bjohansen@hum.ku.dk)
Ph.D. Post.doc. at the Center for European Islamic Thought, University of Copenhagen. Birgitte is a sociologist of religion. Her main work is on secularization, religious minorities and institutional integration.

Dorthe Høvids Possing (hovids@hum.ku.dk)
Ph.D. Candidate at the Minority Studies Section, Institute for Cross-Cultural and Regional Studies, University of Copenhagen. Her current research focuses on young Muslim women in Denmark, Britain and America and their use of the Internet for information retrieval, communication and activism.

Garbi Schmidt (GS@sfi.dk)
Ph.D. Professor of Cultural Encounters at the Institute for Culture and Identity, Roskilde University, Denmark. Garbi's field of expertise is Islamic Studies with a special focus on Muslim minorities in the West and issues of citizenship and integration.

www.ingramcontent.com/pod-product-compliance
Ingram Content Group UK Ltd.
Pitfield, Milton Keynes, MK11 3LW, UK
UKHW021823140426
5217IPUK00004B/58